FRIEND MAKERS & CROWD BREAKERS

Group

Loveland, Colorado

Friend-Makers & Crowdbreakers
Copyright © 1997 Group Publishing, Inc.

CREDITS
Editor: Jan Kershner
Contributing Authors: Jody Brolsma, Vicki Glembocki, Nanette Goings, Susan L. Lingo, Julie Meiklejohn, Amy Nappa, Ann Marie Rozum, Amy Simpson, Mary Van Aalsburg, and Cheryl Voorhis
Managing Editor: Paul Woods
Chief Creative Officer: Joani Schultz
Copy Editor: Janis Sampson
Art Director: Lisa Chandler
Cover Art Director: Helen H. Lannis
Computer Graphic Artist: Joyce Douglas
Cover Designer/Illustrator: Diana Walters
Production Manager: Peggy Naylor

Unless otherwise noted, Scriptures quoted from The Youth Bible, New Century Version, copyright © 1991 by Word Publishing, Dallas, Texas 75039. Used by permission.

Library of Congress Cataloging-in-Publication Data
Friend-makers & crowdbreakers
     p.   cm.
   ISBN 0-7644-2006-2
   1. Christian education--Activity programs. 2. Christian education of children. 3. Games in Christian education. 4. Friendship-
-Biblical teaching--Study and teaching (Elementary) I. Group Publishing.
BV1536.5.F75   1997
268'.432--dc21   97-3358
                                      CIP

10 9 8 7 6 5 4 3 2 1   06 05 04 03 02 01 00 99 98 97

Printed in the United States of America.

Contents

ntroduction

You arrive, full of energy and enthusiasm. They arrive, full of trepidation and apprehension. You have big plans; they have big insecurities. You and your class have a big problem.

Making the most of your time together is what Christian education is all about. At the most, you get only a few hours each week to teach your kids about Jesus and the loving plans he has for their lives.

But it's hard to get your message across when kids aren't interacting, when they're feeling shy, or when they're forming cliques. When you're wasting precious time trying to build teamwork, you're not building faith.

That's where **Friend-Makers & Crowdbreakers** can help.

The crowdbreakers in this book are designed to help your kids get to know each other in no time. The easy, low-prep games and activities are perfect to use with a new group of kids or to spice up a session with kids you've known for years. Either way, these crowdbreakers will help you lead kids to new fun and new friends.

Then what? You know how it is—kids are friends one day, then spatting the next. But fickle friendships aren't what the Bible teaches.

Help your kids form friendships that last—the Bible-based way! **Friend-Makers & Crowdbreakers** will teach kids to look at friendship in a whole new way.

Each friend-maker is based on a Scripture passage that focuses on a biblical quality of friendship or portrays an actual friendship in the Bible. Your kids will be introduced to Barnabas and learn that real friends defend each other. They'll meet Daniel's friends and discover that real friends trust God. They'll turn to Proverbs and find that real friends don't gossip about each other.

And they'll be having so much fun they won't even realize that they're learning important biblical concepts—concepts that will help them develop friendships that last a lifetime.

So join in the fun and fellowship with **Friend-Makers & Crowdbreakers**—and be on your way to fast friendships the Bible-based way!

CROWDBREAKERS

The Jelly Bean Game

Overview: Children will share interesting facts about themselves in this treat-filled getting-acquainted activity!

Supplies: You'll need a bag of jelly beans or fish-shaped crackers.

Have children sit in a circle. Show them the bag of jelly beans and say: **We're going to have a treat! Each of you may take as many jelly beans as you want but don't eat them yet. Just hold them in your hand until I say you can eat them.**

Be sure not to tell children how many jelly beans to take. It's OK if one child takes a handful and another child takes only a few. As you pass out the candy, continue to remind children not to eat the jelly beans just yet.

Once all of the children have jelly beans, take a few candies yourself and join the circle. Say: **We're going to go around the circle and tell the class some interesting facts about ourselves. Before you can eat your jelly beans, you have to tell one fact about yourself for every jelly bean you have in your hand. That means if you have one jelly bean, you only need to tell one thing about yourself. But if you have ten jelly beans, you have to tell us ten things about yourself. Everyone, count your jelly beans!**

Children who have taken a lot of jelly beans will probably moan and groan a bit.

Give the class a few minutes to think of things to say. You can begin the crowdbreaker and help children think of things to say. For instance, say something like, "I'll go first. I have three jelly beans in my hand. My name is Mrs. Brown. I have two brothers, and I have a dog."

After you finish your introduction, say to the child on your right: **Your turn.**

Continue around the circle until each child has had a chance to speak.

Children who have taken lots of jelly beans may have trouble thinking of enough facts to tell. Prompt children by asking questions such as...

- "How old are you?"
- "When is your birthday?"
- "Do you have any brothers or sisters? What are their names?"
- "Do you have any pets?"
- "What's your favorite TV show?"

- "What's your favorite food?"
- "Do you play any sports?"
- "What's your favorite toy?"
- "What's your favorite subject in school?"

When children have all introduced themselves, say: **Now that we know a little bit about everyone here, we can eat our jelly beans!**

The Story of Me

Overview: Children will make Paper Pals with partners and then introduce their new pals to the rest of the class.

Supplies: You'll need newsprint and markers.

Have children form pairs, and give each pair a marker. Give each child a sheet of newsprint that is at least as long as the child is tall.

Say: **We're going to make Paper Pals. Decide in your pair who will go first. The first person will lie down on his or her sheet of paper. The partner will then use a marker to trace around the outline of the person's body. Then switch, and have the other partner trace an outline on the other sheet of paper. Take your time, and be careful not to get any marker ink on your partner's clothes.**

When everyone has finished tracing, pass out a few more markers to each child. Say: **Now draw some things about yourself inside the**

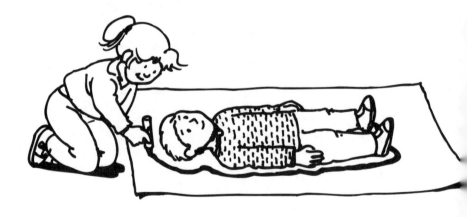

outline of your body. If you have any pets, you could draw them inside your outline. If you play soccer, you might want to draw a soccer ball. If you have brothers or sisters, you could draw pictures of them. You could draw the house you live in or a picture of what you hope to be when you grow up. The only rule is this: Whatever you draw has to describe something about you.

Give children about ten minutes to draw. Walk around the room and offer help and suggestions as needed. After ten minutes, say: **Now take turns describing what you've drawn to your partner. Listen carefully to your partner because you'll get to introduce your partner to the class by describing his or her drawing.**

Then have children stand and introduce their partners to the class by describing their partners' drawings.

Friendship Folders

Overview: Kids will create their own Friendship Folders, then pass them around for others to autograph, fingerprint, or illustrate. This ongoing activity will encourage kids in your group to reach out and get to know each other better.

Supplies: You'll need Bibles, an old wallpaper book (paint and hardware stores give these away), lots of four-by-four inch pieces of plain paper, scissors, a stapler, permanent markers, and pens.

Tell kids they're going to be making Friendship Folders. Have each person select a page from the wallpaper book to use for the front and back covers of a Friendship Folder. Have them trim the covers so they're slightly larger than the pieces of paper.

Demonstrate how to place twelve to fifteen pieces of paper between the covers and then staple the pages inside the covers to form a book. Let kids decorate their covers using permanent markers. Then tell them it's time to mingle!

Encourage kids to greet each other and sign each other's Friendship Folders. They can sign their names, write their favorite Bible verses, or draw pictures. Older kids may want to select Bible verses to call their own. Each person could include the special verse when he or she signs a book. (Not only will kids memorize their own Bible verses, but they'll learn the verses the other kids write as well!)

Pages can be added to the folders by removing the staples and inserting more paper. You may want to have kids make a few extra Friendship Folders to keep in the classroom. Each time you have a guest or new class member, give that person a folder and have the rest of the class sign it.

For extra fun, keep the Friendship Folders in your classroom. Once a month, have kids sign the books with new verses or sayings. You may find that, if given a chance, kids will maintain ongoing conversations in the folders!

"You Are Special!" Sing-Along

Overview: Children will enjoy inviting others to introduce themselves while singing this fun song. At first, you may need to sing alone. But after children hear the song a few times, they'll want to join right in!

Supplies: None

Sing this song to a new child in class or to each child in a new group of children.

You Are Special!
(Tune: "Frère Jacques")

You are special, you are special,
(Child's name), (child's name).
**Tell us news about you. What things do you like to do?
We want to know, we want to know.**

After you sing the song using a child's name, have the child tell the class something he or she enjoys doing. Kids might tell about their hobbies, favorite sports, or favorite subjects in school.

For extra fun, have the class sing back to the child using the information he or she just related. For example, if Tiffany said she likes to play outside, the class could sing:
"You are special, you are special,
Tiffany, Tiffany.
Tiffany likes to play outside. Tiffany likes to play outside.
Now we know, now we know."

Encourage children to make up more verses to the song. It'll spark their creativity and help them get to know each other better! You might use verses such as "What is it you like to eat?" or "What is it you'd like to be?"

Roll Call

Overview: Kids will get to know each other better in this fun, fast-paced way to take attendance.

Supplies: None

Have kids sit in a line of chairs and number off down the line. (Be sure you have a number too.) Tell kids they'll need to remember their numbers to play this game.

Teach kids this easy six-beat rhythm: Slap your lap twice, clap twice, then snap the fingers of your right hand and then your left hand. Lead kids in the rhythm until they're comfortable and confident with it.

As you lead the rhythm, say your number as you snap the fingers of your right hand. Then while snapping the fingers of your left hand, say the number of one of the kids in the line. The person whose number you call will try to keep in rhythm and say his or her number and the number of another person in line during the next sequence. That person will continue the process.

If someone doesn't respond to his or her number or gets out of rhythm, that person moves to the end of the line and each person moves up one chair. So each person's number will change regularly!

This game can go on as long as you wish with no one ever having to leave the game. And if kids think this game is getting too easy, speed it up!

Bunch of Buddies

Overview: Use this craft idea with a new group of children, and each child will feel like one of the bunch!

Supplies: You'll need a T-shirt for each child. You'll also need fabric paints or fabric markers and some scrap cardboard.

Before this activity, you can purchase a T-shirt for each child, or you can ask each child to bring in a plain T-shirt. If children bring their own T-shirts, you may want to have a few extra shirts available for those who forget.

As children arrive, give each one a T-shirt. Help children use the fabric paints or markers to write the name of your class and perhaps a motto or a Bible verse on the front of their T-shirts. Then have each child write his or her name in small letters on the back of the T-shirt.

Encourage children to be creative in the way they write their names. They may want to write with their favorite colors or draw small, simple pictures next to their names.

When children have finished writing their names on their T-shirts, say: **Now I'd like you to go around and introduce yourself to every other person in the room. As you introduce yourself to someone, have that person write his or her name on the back of your T-shirt.**

Buddy Builder

Be sure to put a piece of cardboard between the front and the back of each T-shirt so the paint or marker doesn't bleed through.

When each child has signed each T-shirt, allow the T-shirts to dry. Then have children take the T-shirts home as reminders of the new friends they met in class. You may want to have kids wear their T-shirts on special class occasions in the future.

This activity also works well with other objects the children can personalize, such as posters, plastic cups, or tote bags.

If the Shoe Fits...

Overview: In this simple game, kids will learn more about themselves and each other.

Supplies: You'll need four signs that read "Sports Shoes," "Dress Shoes," "Casual Shoes," and "Hiking Boots."

Before class, hang the four signs in the room, one on each wall.

When kids arrive, point out the signs on the walls. Say: **As a way of getting to know each other better, I want you each to answer this question: If you were a pair of shoes, what kind of shoes would you be? When you've decided what kind of shoes you would be, go stand under the sign that describes that kind of shoe.**

When kids have chosen their types of shoes and are standing under the appropriate signs, have them introduce themselves to the other kids standing under the same sign. If one person is alone under a sign, join him or her. If more than one person is alone, pair those kids into a group.

Then say: **Now, one at a time, tell the rest of your group why you chose the type of shoe you did.** Give kids a few minutes to share with each other, then direct each group to form a circle.

Say: **Now introduce the person on your right to the rest of the class, and tell why he or she chose that type of shoe.**

Give kids a few moments to refresh their memories. Then ask each person to introduce the person on his or her right to the rest of the class.

Musical Handshakes

Overview: In this active musical game, kids will have fun introducing themselves to others.

Supplies: You'll need a cassette or CD of upbeat, lively praise music and a cassette or CD player.

Have kids form two equal groups. Have one group form a circle, facing out. Have the other group form a circle around the first group, facing in.

Tell kids that while the music plays, kids in the inner circle are to walk clockwise, and kids in the outer circle are to walk counterclockwise. When the music stops, kids should stop walking and face a partner from the other circle. Partners will shake hands, say their names, and tell one interesting fact about themselves. Kids might say what sports they like or how many brothers or sisters they have. Then the music will start again.

> **Buddy Builder**
>
> To add variety to this activity, give kids a different action to complete each time the music stops. For instance, they could give each other high fives, shake hands, or clap three times.

For extra fun, encourage kids to try to name a new fact each time the music stops. After the activity, have each person introduce a new friend to the class by naming one fact he or she learned about that friend.

Find Me!

Overview: Kids will have a great time getting to know each other in this fun, rather noisy activity!

Supplies: You'll need blindfolds for all the kids.

Before class, move furniture to the sides of the room and remove any other obstacles from the center of the room.

Buddy Builder

If kids are stumped trying to think of word pairs, offer suggestions such as "macaroni and cheese," "day and night," or "hand and glove."

Have kids line up into two rows, facing each other. Let each person shake hands with a partner from the other row.

Tell partners to think of two words that go together, such as "peanut" and "butter" or "sock" and "shoe." Each pair will need its own set of words. When partners have agreed on two words, have each partner choose one of the words.

Then have the two rows of kids go to opposite sides of the room. Tell kids that they'll all be blindfolded and will have to find their partners by calling out the words their partners chose. Further explain that each

Peanut...   ...Butter.

person will be walking around the room, calling his or her partner's word until that partner is found. Remind kids to walk in the "bumpers-up" position—hands up and palms facing forward—to avoid injury.

Have kids put on the blindfolds and try to find their partners.

When partners find each other, have them take off their blindfolds, shake hands, and tell each other their names plus one interesting fact about themselves.

After the game, have kids introduce their partners to the rest of the class.

Have a Ball!

Overview: In this fun memory game, kids will toss more than names around!

Supplies: You'll need at least one soft, throwable object for each person.

Have kids stand in a circle. Begin by introducing everyone in the circle. Then toss a foam ball or other soft object to someone else, saying that person's name as you do so. That person will then toss the ball to someone else in the circle and say that person's name. Kids can continue tossing the ball around the circle until everyone has tossed the ball and it is returned to you. Try the passing pattern again, with each person tossing to the same person he or she tossed the ball to the first time.

After kids have figured out the pattern, introduce more balls, one at a time, to the pattern. Each person will pass all of the balls in the same pattern as the first time, saying the recipient's name with each toss. Continue playing as long as kids like—but beware!—the pace will pick up quickly and laughs are likely to erupt.

For extra fun, try the pattern backward, with each person passing to the person they caught the ball from in the original pattern.

Partners From the Past

Overview: Children will be encouraged to interact as they learn about familiar biblical characters in this game.

Supplies: You'll need a pen, paper, and scissors.

Before this activity, think of biblical characters who are typically recognized as pairs. For example, you might choose Adam and Eve, Cain and Abel, Ruth and Naomi, and David and Goliath.

Cut a slip of paper for each student, then write the name of a biblical character on each paper slip. Make sure that for each name you write on a slip, you prepare another slip with the name of the character's "partner." If there is an uneven number of students, you can join in this game too!

As students arrive, give each child a prepared paper slip. Tell children to keep their characters' identities secret until the game begins.

When all the children have gathered, tell them that they're each going to search for a Partner From the Past to discover whose biblical character would be a match for their own. Tell children that there's only one rule: They each must find a Partner From the Past by asking only yes-or-no questions. Have children mingle and ask each other fact-finding questions.

As children find their partners, they may sit down.

For extra fun, try one of the following variations:

● Allow younger children to announce their characters' names while milling about, and then have them each listen for the name which would be a match.

● Tell older children they must each find a Partner From the Past by first guessing which book of the Bible the character is found in.

Buddy Builder

This activity is based on your children's knowledge of biblical characters. Choose characters that match the level of knowledge your students have about the Bible. You may want to reinforce lessons by choosing characters you've recently studied.

Spaghetti Gumdrop Creations

Overview: In this creative activity, kids will build more than sculptures—they'll begin building friendships, too!

Supplies: You'll need gumdrops and uncooked spaghetti.

Have kids form groups of no more than four. Give each group a bag of gumdrops and a handful of uncooked spaghetti. Say: **In your group, find out whose birthday is the closest to today. Then have that person hold one gumdrop in his or her hand.** Pause for kids to follow your instructions.

Then continue: **Now take turns telling the others in your group about the best vacation you've ever had. After you tell about your vacation, poke the end of a piece of spaghetti into the gumdrop. Then pass the creation to someone else in your group, who will do the same. After everyone has told about a vacation and added a piece of spaghetti, add a gumdrop to one of the spaghetti "spines." Then I'll call out another topic for you to tell about, and you'll add spaghetti to the new gumdrop. Let's keep sharing and watching our creations grow!**

Call out instructions such as…

- "Tell about the weirdest thing your mom or dad ever did."
- "Tell about the best amusement park ride you've ever been on."
- "Tell a joke."
- "Tell about your favorite pet or one you'd like to have."
- "Tell about the grossest thing you ever had to eat."

Encourage kids to think of other topics to discuss as they add to their creations. At the end of the activity, have each group display its creation. If you have time, have each child tell one thing he or she learned about someone else in the group.

Bop & Pop

Overview: Kids will get things popping in this musical crowd-breaker.

Supplies: You'll need at least one paper slip and one balloon for each person in your group. You'll also need a cassette or CD of lively music and a cassette or CD player.

Before this activity, write questions on slips of paper. Use questions such as "What's your favorite candy?" or "What's your pet's name? Why?" or "What do you like best about your best friend?" You'll need at least one question for each person.

Before class, roll up the paper slips, and put one paper slip inside a balloon for each person. Blow up and tie off the balloons.

Gather kids in a circle. Hold up a balloon, and say: **This game is like the game Hot Potato. I'll play some music, and we'll bop a balloon around the circle. When the music stops, whoever was the last person to touch the balloon will have to pop the balloon, read the question inside, and answer it. Ready?**

Play a cassette of upbeat music while kids bop the balloon. Turn off the cassette player, and have the last person who touched the balloon pop it in a silly way such as sitting on it, stomping on it, laying on it, or squishing it between his or her knees.

When the person has popped the balloon and answered the question inside, bring out a new balloon and play again. If a student is caught with a balloon twice, have him or her choose someone else to pop the balloon. Then both kids can answer the question. Play until each student has had a chance to pop a balloon and answer a question.

Cereal Scramble

Overview: In this activity, kids will snack, yak, and practice their spelling—all at the same time!

Supplies: You'll need small cups, paper plates, and Alpha-Bits.

Give each person a small cupful of Alpha-Bits. Let kids form pairs, and give each pair a paper plate. Say: **On your plate, use your cereal and your partner's cereal to spell out the name of candy that you both like.** After about thirty seconds, call time, and have pairs take turns calling out the name of the candy they spelled. Each time partners spell a word, instruct each person to eat one of the letters.

Then give pairs a new topic to spell, such as a favorite restaurant, least favorite food, or favorite sports team. As the dwindling "alphabet" makes spelling a challenge, allow pairs to join with other pairs to pool their resources. After a few rounds, distribute new letters, and ask kids to form new pairs to play again.

Who's Behind the Mask?

Overview: Kids will combine their artistic and social skills in this mask-making activity.

Supplies: You'll need paper plates, tape, craft sticks, and markers or crayons.

Set out the supplies. Have each person draw a self-portrait on the front of a paper plate. Then show kids how to tape a craft stick to the back of the plate to make a hand-held mask.

Say: **On the back of your mask, list five interesting facts about yourself. You might list things such as "I like purple bubble gum," "I have a dog named Kitty," or "I have four brothers and a sister." Just don't write your name!**

As kids complete their lists, have them place their masks in a pile on the floor. When all of the masks are finished, have each person choose a mask from the pile and join the circle. Then let each person take a turn holding the mask in front of his or her face and reading aloud the list on the back of the mask. Kids will try to guess whose mask the person is holding.

Just Like Me!

Overview: In this simple crowdbreaker that takes no preparation, children will discover that they have a lot in common.

Supplies: None

Tell the class that you're going to ask a question. Explain to children that they'll have ten seconds to call out their answers and form a group with others who called out the same answer. When children are in these smaller groups, have them introduce themselves to each other. If a child doesn't find a "match," allow that child to suggest the next question.

To get you started, here are a few crowdbreaker questions:

- **What's your favorite kind of sandwich?**
- **What's your favorite subject in school?**
- **What's your favorite vacation spot?**
- **What's your favorite movie?**
- **What's your favorite food at McDonald's?**
- **What kind of car would you like to have?**
- **What kind of pet do you wish you had?**

For extra fun, have one small group perform a simple task such as sing "Happy Birthday to You" to another group, after each question.

What's Your Number?

Overview: Kids will use fun, phony dollars to answer getting-to-know-you questions.

Supplies: You'll need photocopies of the "Pass the Buck" handout on page 22.

Before this activity, photocopy the "Pass the Buck" handout (p. 22), and cut apart the dollar bills. Write a different six-digit serial number on each dollar. Prepare a pretend dollar for each person in class.

Have kids form groups of three. Hand each child a pretend dollar and each trio a "Pass the Buck" questionnaire. Say: **This game is a great way to get to know each other. Look at your dollar bill—do you see the little numbers? Those are called serial numbers, and all dollar bills have them. Serial numbers help us know more about dollar bills, such as when and where they were made.**

Today we're going to use the serial numbers on these pretend dollar bills to learn more about each other. Look at the first digit in your serial number. Now look on the handout until you find that same digit, and follow the directions. Then let someone else in your group take a turn. When everyone has answered a question, we'll switch groups.

After everyone has had a turn answering a question on the handout, have kids form new trios. Be sure each trio has a list of questions. Then kids can use the second digits in their serial numbers for this round. If time allows, kids can play up to six rounds, using different digits each time.

Close by affirming everyone's individuality with comments such as "I'm glad we have so many interesting friends in our group" and "Let's make it a point to get to know each other even better in the following weeks."

If you have time, hand out pencils, and let kids collect autographs on their dollar bills. Then suggest that they use the dollars as bookmarks in their Bibles to remind them of their new friends.

PASS THE BUCK

Questions

- What is **1** of your favorite holiday memories?
- What are **2** things you're proud of?
- What are your **3** favorite foods?
- Which **4** colors of the rainbow are your favorites?
- Where were you living when you were **5** years old?
- Clap someone's hand **6** times.
- If you were on an island, what **7** things would you miss most?
- What's the best thing you ever "**8**"?
- Tap your foot **9** times, then shake someone's hand.
- What would you like to be wearing if the temperature here were below **0**?

Rumble Seat Ramble

Overview: Kids will travel in pretend cars and discover lots of fun facts about the people around them.

Supplies: You'll need a chair for each person. If your group is very large, you may use paper plate "chairs" instead.

Arrange the chairs so they make several "cars." Each car should have two "front seats" and two "back seats." The number of cars will depend on the number of students you have in class. Just make sure there are enough seats for all of the kids. Arrange cars in a line of "traffic," leaving at least three feet between cars.

Have each person choose a car seat and sit down. Say: **Everyone is sitting in a pretend car. Raise your hand if you're in the front seat.** Pause. **Honk your horn if you're the driver.** By the way kids are seated, they should understand who's the driver, who's in the back seat, and so on.

Say: **I'll give you directions about changing seats within your own car or another car. Riders at the end of the line can switch with riders at the front of the line. Also, you'll have to tell something about yourself, so listen closely. We'll see how far you travel and what car you end the game riding in.**

Read aloud the list below. When you've read all the directions, call time.

● **Each rider move one car behind you and tell the passenger beside you your name and age. Go.**

● **Each back-seat rider, switch places within your own car and** tell the driver your favorite color. Go.

● Everyone find a new car to ride in. Then tell someone beside you your least favorite vegetable and why you dislike it. Go.

● Each passenger next to a driver, shake hands with someone in your car and introduce yourself. Then switch places with that person. Go.

● Each passenger and driver find a new car to ride in, then tell two people nearest you where you'd go on your dream vacation.

After the game, gather everyone together, and ask each person to name the most interesting fact discovered about a new friend. Challenge kids to see if they can remember everyone's name.

Bound to Say Hello

Overview: Kids will greet and meet new friends in fun cooperative ways.

Supplies: You'll need medium-sized rubber bands, index cards, and markers.

Older kids will love this fun way to greet each other. Have kids form pairs, and hand each pair an index card, marker, and two rubber bands. Instruct partners to face each other and slip the rubber bands over their wrists to join left hands to right hands.

Say: **Saying hello seems pretty simple, doesn't it? But today we're going to give that plain old hello a new twist! I'll give you a series of directions for saying hello to your partner or to another pair of friends. We'll see if you can work together to greet each other in some new ways. Be sure to keep your wrists joined during the entire activity. Ready? Here we go.**

Read the following list of instructions for kids to greet each other. Allow enough time for each pair to accomplish the tasks.

● **Wave to three other pairs. Use different hands each time you wave.**

● **Give your partner a pat on the back and introduce yourself.**

● **Walk to two other pairs of friends, then shake hands. Tell everyone your name.**

● **Write the words, "Glad to meet you!" on your index card. Each partner must sign his or her name to the card. Then present the card to another pair of friends.**

- **Tap your partner's shoe and tell one thing you like to do in your spare time.**
- **Find another pair of friends and bow to say hello. Tell that pair your names.**

If you have time, invite each pair of kids to invent another new way to say hello, either to each other or to another pair of friends.

Name-Chain Tag

Overview: Kids will learn each other's names in short order during this lively game!

Supplies: None

Gather kids in a group, and invite them to introduce themselves. Then say: **Let's play a game of Name-Chain Tag. I'll choose someone to be "It." It can only tag someone whose name he or she calls out. Then that person links arms with It. The "new link" in the "chain" becomes the only one who can tag another person—and only if he or she calls out that person's name. We'll see how quickly we can attach everyone in the group to our human name chain!**

Play the game through once, coaching kids who have trouble remembering names. Then play again, but this time let the kids on either end of the chain tag people and call out names. If space is limited have kids hop, walk, or tiptoe instead of run.

If there's time when the game is over, gather everyone in groups of three and create a "quiet chain." Have kids each introduce themselves and tell one interesting personal fact such as a favorite sports car or the number of family members.

Buddy Builder

If your kids are completely unfamiliar with each other, you might want to have each child wear a name tag during this activity.

Then invite trios to join another group and repeat their important information. Continue until all the trios have joined to make one large group. Finish by challenging kids to see who can name everyone in the entire group—and the interesting facts each one told.

Pizza Pizazz

Overview: Kids will love making dessert pizzas at the Friendship Pizzeria.

Supplies: You'll need napkins, canned icing, plastic knives, raisins, candied fruits, chocolate chips, peanuts, or gumdrops. You'll also need a plain sugar cookie for each child. If you plan to use gumdrops, you may want to use scissors to snip them into thirds for colorful candy "slices."

Set out the "pizza" ingredients in the following order: cookies, icing, toppings, and napkins. Gather kids near the ingredients table and say: **Welcome to Friendship Pizzeria. This is our newly opened pretend cafe that specializes in delicious pizzas and fun friendships. Two of the best ways to get to know others is by working with them and eating with them. And today we'll have the chance to do both. Let's form three groups.** Pause while kids form three small groups. Number groups from one to three.

Say: **Group One, you're the Spreaders. You'll spread icing on the cookie pizzas. Group Two, you'll be the Terrific Toppers. You'll add toppings to the mini-pizzas. And Group Three, you'll be the Sweet Servers, who'll place the pizzas on napkins and set them at the opposite end of the room to eat later.**

As you work, keep your ears tuned because when I say, "sweet switch," each person must change to a new group and job. That way everyone will have a chance to work in all three groups and meet even more new friends! Ready? Let's go to work!

Be sure to call "sweet switch" three times. When the cookie pizzas are finished, invite kids to eat at the Friendship Pizzeria and chat with their new friends. Encourage kids to ask their new friends getting-to-know-you questions such as "How old are you?" "What's your favorite part of school?" and "What do you like to do?"

Sticks and Stones...
and Feathers Too!

Overview: In this two-fold activity, children will get the opportunity to share a bit about themselves and then play a fun game with partners.

Supplies: For each person, you'll need a stick, a small stone, and a feather.

Place the sticks, stones, and feathers in the center of the room; and seat children in a circle around the items. Say: **It's often hard to meet everyone and learn something about people in a group. This activity will help us learn more about each other and have fun while learning. See the items in the center of the circle? Come choose an item that best tells about you.**

For example, you might choose a speckled stone because you have freckles. Or maybe you like a certain feather because you have a bird as a pet at home. Then we'll go around the room, and you can introduce yourself and tell why you picked that item.

Allow time for everyone to choose an item. Then ask for volunteers to tell their names and why they chose the items. When everyone has had a turn to share, say: **Now we can play a funny game to learn even more about each other. You'll each need a stick, a stone, and a feather to play this game. You'll also need to find a partner.** Be sure everyone has three items from the center of the room. If there's an uneven number of children, make one group of three.

Say: **Sit on the floor cross-legged, and place the items in front of you. When I count to three, choose one of your items and place it between you and your partner. If your partner chose a feather, you must tell one thing that tickles you or makes you laugh. If your partner chose a stick, tell one thing that pokes at you or makes you angry. And if your partner chose a stone, tell one thing that's hard for you to do.** Count to three, then allow time for partners to share. Repeat the game several more times, then have kids find new partners.

When children have finished playing, let them take their feathers, sticks, and stones home as reminders of their new friends.

Name-Card Scramble

Overview: In this series of active name-recognition games, kids will get to identify new friends by name, by voice—even by feet!

Supplies: You'll need markers and index cards.

Hand each child an index card. Have kids write their names in large letters on their cards and then decorate their name cards with funny self-portraits. Be sure each child prepares a name card. As children work, explain that the name cards will be used to play a variety of getting-to-know-you games. When kids have finished making the cards, have them introduce themselves briefly as they hold up the cards they made. Then play the following games:

● **ABC Me!** Shuffle the name cards, and scatter them at the front of the room. When you say "go," have kids hop forward, snatch a card, then see how quickly they can arrange themselves in ABC order according to the names on their cards. (Kids shouldn't choose their own cards from the pile.) When everyone is in alphabetical order, read the names aloud. Then have kids find the people whose name cards they're holding and personally introduce themselves with handshakes.

● **Speak Up!** Have kids form a circle, holding their name cards in plain sight. Go around the circle and have everyone say his or her name in a distinctive style. For example, a name could be sung or whispered or made to go up and down in tone.

Continue around the circle three times, having each person repeat his or her name in the same style as in the previous round. Then scramble the name cards face down in the center of the circle. Invite each person to select a name card and try to repeat the name in the style it was said and identify the person belonging to the name card.

● **What a "Feet"!** For this "feat" of memory, have everyone remove one shoe and place it in the center of the room. Pass out the name cards, and make sure no one is holding his or her own card. Challenge each student to find the person whose name is on the card and then bring that person his or her missing shoe. Encourage kids to introduce themselves as the shoes are returned.

Never-Ever Peanuts

Overview: Kids will have fun trading real peanuts in this "nutty" getting-to-know-you game.

Supplies: You'll need a bag of peanuts in the shell.

Hand each person five peanuts in the shell. Then have kids form two concentric circles, with the outer one facing in and the inner one facing out. Make sure circles have equal numbers of kids.

Say: **In this game, I'll tell you how many spaces to move to the**

left or right. The person you're standing across from in the other circle will be your partner. I'll give you a "never-ever instruction" such as "Name a food you've never, ever eaten." You'll tell your partner a food you've never eaten. For example, you could say, "I've never, ever eaten a chocolate butterfly." Then trade a peanut with your partner. Then we'll walk around the circle, and you'll have a new partner for the next never-ever instruction.

Begin the game by telling everyone to move three steps to the right. The inner circle will move in one direction, and the outer circle will move in the opposite direction. Then give a never-ever instruction from the list below. Continue rotating the circles, and giving new directions until you've used all the never-ever instructions. If there's time, allow kids to make up their own never-ever instructions.

● **Name a place you've never, ever visited.**
● **Tell the name of an animal you've never, ever seen.**
● **What kind of car have you never, ever ridden in?**

- **What's a food you've never, ever eaten?**
- **Who is someone you've never, ever met?**
- **Give the name of a noise you've never, ever heard.**
- **Tell the name of a friend you've never, ever written to.**
- **What's a toy you've always wanted but never, ever had?**
- **What kind of pet would you never, ever want?**

After the game, have kids form a large circle and enjoy their peanuts as they tell fun facts they learned about each other during the game.

Color Kaleidoscope

Overview: Kids will work together to make colorful kaleidoscopes that tell about themselves.

Supplies: You'll need construction paper scraps, tape or glue sticks, markers, scissors, plastic drinking straws, and two twenty-two-inch poster board circles.

Before class, cut a hole in the center of each poster board circle. Make sure the hole is large enough for a drinking straw to slip through, allowing the circle to spin on the straw.

Have kids form two groups, and give each group a poster board circle and a plastic drinking straw. Say: **A kaleidoscope is a round tube you look through to see beautiful colors and shapes that twirl and change before your eyes. In your groups, you're going to make kaleidoscopes that tell about each of you. Think of a colorful shape that tells something about you. For example, a red tulip might show how much you enjoy flowers or a blue car might mean you want to be a race-car driver when you grow up. You can cut out a shape or shapes and glue them to your group's kaleidoscope circle. Then write your name on the shape you made.**

Allow time for kids to create their kaleidoscopes. When both kaleidoscopes are finished, have kids sit in two groups. Slide the drinking straws through the holes in the center of the poster board circles.

Say: **Have one person from your group hold your kaleidoscope. Then someone from the other group will spin the wheel and point to it. When the kaleidoscope wheel stops spinning, the person whose name and shape are closest to the person's finger must stand up and tell his or her name and what the shape represents. Then that person can come spin the wheel of the** other group. **We'll continue until everyone's had a chance to spin a kaleidoscope and share.**

By the end of this activity, kids will have met their classmates and discovered some of their interests and dreams. You may want to display the kaleidoscopes in a hallway or on a bulletin board for everyone to enjoy.

Paper Pals

Overview: In this crazy scavenger hunt, children will be tickled to their funny bones—and meet lots of friends.

Supplies: You'll need markers, tape, index cards, scissors, and photocopies of the "Build-a-Body Friends" handout from page 32.

Before this activity, photocopy the "Build-a-Body Friends" handout on colored construction paper, and cut out the body parts. Be sure there's a head and a set of arms, legs, and feet for each child.

Give each child an index card, marker, and seven of the same body part. For example, hand one child seven right arms, another child seven heads, another child seven left feet, and so on. Have children write their names on the backs of the paper parts.

Say: **Greeting and meeting new friends is sometimes awkward—but today it's going to be especially fun! As you greet and meet new people, you'll be assembling a paper friend to remind you of the friends in our class. Each of you has an index-card body and seven of the same body part. Your challenge is to meet six friends and trade paper body parts to complete a pretend friend. Tape each body part to your index-card body as you go. When your paper friend is complete, it will have the names of six real friends on the back!**

Let children collect the pieces they need to complete the paper friends. Encourage children to introduce themselves as they trade paper body parts. When all the paper friends have been constructed, either send them home as reminders of how much fun it is meeting new people, or create colorful hanging mobiles of the "friends."

BUILD-A-BODY FRIENDS

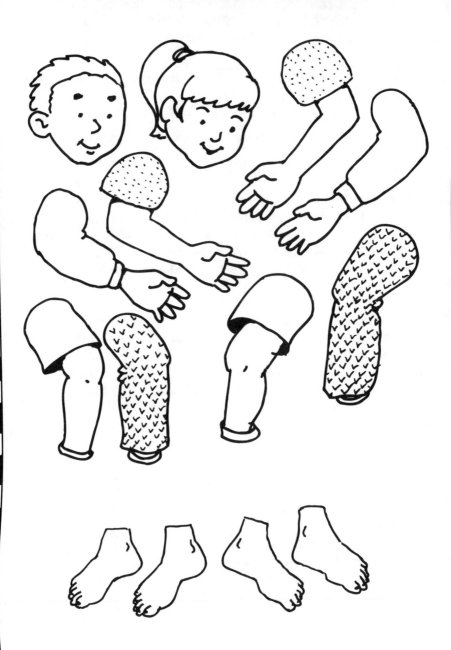

Crazy Costumes

Overview: In this game, kids will learn to remember each other's names in interesting ways.

Supplies: You'll need a variety of wild wearable items such as a crazy hat, gloves, mittens, a colorful necklace, a wild scarf, a belt, a goofy tie, zany sunglasses, and earmuffs. The wilder the items, the more fun the game!

Place the wearable items in the center of the floor. Gather kids in a circle around the items and say: **It's easier to remember someone's name when you associate that person with an object. For example, if I put on this crazy hat and tell you my name** (don the hat and tell your name), **you'll probably remember my name easier even when I'm not wearing the hat.** Remove the hat.

Let's go around the circle. When it's your turn, put on one or two crazy items and say, "I'm (name) and I like to wear my (object name or names). Then return the items to the pile. The next person must put on your items and repeat your name, then don new items and say his or her own name. The next person must repeat the costumes and names of the first two people, then add his or her own name and costume. We'll see how many people's names and costumes we can remember in a row!

If you have young children, encourage them to wear only one item at a time or repeat only one person's name. Older kids may enjoy the challenge of remembering entire ensembles!

Rainbow Friendship Streamers

Overview: Younger children will especially love this getting-to-know-you craft game.

Supplies: You'll need colorful crepe paper, scissors, markers, small rubber bands, and cardboard tubes. Empty bathroom tissue tubes or wrapping paper tubes cut into four-inch sections work well for this activity. If you can't collect enough tubes, make them from poster board.

Before this activity, be sure you have one tube for each child. You'll also need to cut ten twelve-inch crepe paper streamers for each child.

Hand each child a cardboard tube, ten crepe paper streamers, and a small rubber band. Show children how to slide a rubber band on one end of the tube. Then have each child write his or her name on the ten crepe paper streamers. Say: **Meeting new friends is fun and brings lots of smiles. You can think of new friends as rainbows—bright, cheery, and full of friendly promise! Let's**

make Rainbow Friendship Streamers to remind us how fun it is to meet new friends.

Go around the room and meet ten new friends. Tell them your name and listen to their names. Then trade a paper streamer with your new friend and slide it under your rubber band. When you're finished collecting streamers, we'll raise a cheer for our new friendships!

Allow plenty of time for children to greet and meet each other and trade streamers. When all the streamers have been exchanged, lead kids in the following cheers. Encourage them to repeat the cheers several times as they wave and rustle their Rainbow Friendship Streamers.

Cheer One:
F-r-i-e-n-d-s,
Let's raise a cheer for friend-li-ness!

Cheer Two:
Meet and greet new friends today.
Friends will make you smile and say:
"I'm so happy I could fly—
Wave your streamers to the sky!"

Real Icebreakers

Overview: Kids will relish these hot-weather crowdbreakers! Use these as kickoff activities for VBS and other special warm-weather programs.

Supplies: You'll need a bag of ice cubes.

Gather kids outside into two or three circles. Say: **Did you know that games designed to help you meet people or learn their names are called icebreakers? Today we're going to play a couple of fun icebreakers using real ice cubes!**

The first game is called Icy Handshakes. I'll give one person in each circle an ice cube. That person places the ice cube in the palm of his or her right hand, then shakes hands with a neighbor. They introduce themselves to each other, and the ice cube is passed to the neighbor's palm. Continue the icy handshakes and introductions around the circle until the ice cube is completely melted. Then sit down.

Hand one person in each circle an ice cube, and have them begin the icy handshakes. When everyone is sitting down, say: **That was some really cool fun! Now let's try another icebreaker. Form groups of four or five.** Pause for kids to form their groups. Then say: **In this game, you'll be tossing an ice cube back and forth as quickly as you can. When the ice cube comes to you, say your name first, then say the name of someone else in the group, and quickly toss the ice cube to that person. See how many times you can toss the ice cube before it melts.**

Hand one person in each group an ice cube, and begin the game. After the ice cubes are melted, you may wish to treat kids to icy cold Fruit Cubes. To prepare the cubes, simply freeze fruit juice in ice cube trays. Serve each child two or three icy treats in a paper cup.

I've Got a Secret

Overview: In this fun guessing game, kids will learn each other's names and discover "secrets" that make each person special.

Supplies: None

elp kids find partners. Tell each person to think of a "secret"—secrets shouldn't be anything too personal, but should just be fun facts about themselves that others can guess. Special talents they have and weird foods they enjoy are fun facts for kids to share.

Say: **Don't say your secret out loud. Your partner will try to guess what your special secret is by asking yes-or-no questions. After two minutes, I'll call time. If your partner hasn't guessed correctly by that time, you may tell your secret. Then you'll switch roles with your partner.** Call time after two minutes, and have partners switch roles. Then say: **I'm sure you've all learned lots of fun facts about each other. Let's share those facts!**

Have kids introduce their partners to the rest of the class. For example, Matt might say, "This is my partner Chris, and his secret is that he was born in England."

No-Lose Musical Chairs

Overview: Children will play a game that's an old favorite but with a new twist that makes everybody a winner.

Supplies: You'll need chairs, a cassette or CD of lively music, and a cassette or CD player.

usical Chairs has been a favorite game of children for generations, dating back to the days of parlor games. In the traditional version of the game, the object is to have one winner and many losers. In this more cooperative approach, the excitement is just as intense but without the tears of the losers. Children can play this game in same-age or multi-age groups. Choose good sturdy chairs that can support considerable weight. Select music that is lively and especially fun for children.

The game starts in the usual way with one less chair than the number of players. Set the chairs in a large circle with the children standing on the inside of the circle.

Say: **When the music starts, march clockwise around the circle in single file. When the music stops, hurry to a chair and sit down. But don't leave anyone out. The group's goal is to make sure everyone is sitting somewhere. Make room for the person without a chair.**

Play the music for about twenty seconds, then stop without warning.

The children will scramble for chairs, and one person will be left with nowhere to sit. He or she will quickly share the nearest chair with the child already sitting there.

Remove a chair, adjust the shape of the circle, and start the music for a second round. Repeat this process over and over, removing a chair each time, adjusting the circle as it becomes smaller and smaller, but *never* removing a player. Children will have to share the remaining chairs.

At the final round, all of the children will be left circling the one remaining chair. Trying to get everyone on that chair will require a real "piling technique" which will give the game a hilarious ending.

In this "everybody-wins" approach, the laughter and fun will far surpass that of the original game, and children will develop new attitudes of cooperation. And who knows? They may want to invent ways of turning other competitive games into more "friend-friendly" activities.

Sock Hop Scramble

Overview: In this crowdbreaker, kids will use what they have plenty of—energy and old socks!

Supplies: You'll need a supply of old socks, a dark-colored permanent marker, paper, tape, a cassette or CD of fifties music, and a cassette or CD player.

Gather the assortment of old socks. You'll need one sock for each student in class. (You might ask kids to bring in old socks from home. Most families have plenty to spare!)

Choose one of the options detailed at the end of this activity, depending on the age and skill level of the kids in your class. Directions are given for each of the options.

Before class, cut a two-inch square of white or light-colored paper for each student. Depending on the option you chose, draw a shape, simple picture, number, or single letter of the alphabet on each paper square. Tape a paper square on the top of each sock's toe.

Have kids form a circle. Put the labeled socks in a pile in the center of the circle. Have each person choose one sock and slip it on so the taped square can be seen by everyone. If the socks are large enough, kids can put them on over their shoes. Otherwise, have kids remove their shoes and put the socks on for a real sock hop atmosphere.

Say: **Back in the 1950s, people used to hold sock hops where all the teenagers danced in their stocking feet. I'm going to play a little sock hop music right now. As soon as the music stops, hurry to find a partner whose paper square matches your own.** Give kids directions on how to match squares, depending on which option you chose when making the squares.

After kids find partners, have them exchange names and each tell one interesting personal fact. Then start the music, and let kids play again. Or you may want to let younger children simply "dance" or hop around in a circle.

Options for this activity are listed below. The suggestions explain what to draw on the paper squares and how to match the squares. Feel free to come up with ideas of your own.

● **Shape or Picture Option.** Younger children will appreciate having shapes or simple pictures on their paper squares. That way they can easily match squares identical to their own. Make sure to make at least two of each shape or picture so everyone can find a partner.

● **Number Option.** Older children will enjoy mathematical challenges using numbers. Each student can find a partner by adding the number on the paper square to another's number to get a predetermined total. For example, you might choose a total of twelve. You'll need to make sock labels with two of each numeral from zero through twelve.

● **Letter Option.** For larger groups of older children, select several words for partners to spell. For example, have partners spell "friend," which would put six children in a group using the single letters f-r-i-e-n-d. Or use the word "love," which would group four children, and so on. Of course, you need to make enough letters to spell each of the words you have chosen. Be sure to write the words in large letters on a chalkboard or newsprint so kids can see the correct spelling.

FRIEND-MAKERS

What's Mine Is Yours

Friendly Focus: Real friends share their belongings.

Scripture: 1 Samuel 18:1-4

Overview: By delivering snacks to each other, kids will learn that God wants us to share with others in the same way he shares with us.

Preparation: You'll need a Bible, at least five plastic bowls, and snacks such as a favorite dry cereal, popcorn, and different flavors of sugarless candy. You'll also need a method of differentiating which bowl belongs to which group of kids. For example, you might use colored bowls, or you might put a different sticker on each bowl.

THE FUN

Have kids form at least five groups. There can be as few as two students in each group. (If you have fewer than ten students, form fewer groups.) Have each group either sit in a circle on the floor or sit at its own table. Give each group a bowl of snacks. Tell students not to eat any of the goodies until the game is over.

Say: **The Bible tells us to share everything we have with one another. We're going to practice that right now.**

Have each group choose one person to be the first Deliverer. Explain that when you say "go," a Deliverer from each group will deliver its bowl of snacks to another group. As soon as a group's Deliverer sits back down, the Deliverer from that group should jump up and deliver the bowl of snacks that was just received.

Keep in mind these two rules: No group should ever end up with its original bowl of snacks, and there should only be one bowl of snacks per group at any time. Everyone will have a turn to scramble in this game! When you say, "Stop!" each group should have a bowl of snacks.

If desired, play some lively music as the kids dash from group to group. After about two minutes, turn off the music and call time.

THE FELLOWSHIP

Have kids sit in a circle. Choose a student to read aloud 1 Samuel 18:1-4. Ask:

● **How did you feel about giving your snacks away in this activity?**

● **Why do you think God wants us to share?**

● **Do you think God blesses us when we share? In what way?**

- **What do you think would happen if everyone in the world shared the way we just did?**

Say: **God takes care of us, and he wants us to take care of each other. In our activity, you didn't need to worry about not having any snacks left because when you shared with another group someone else shared with you. Remember, real friends share their belongings. That's what God wants us to do. Let's enjoy the treats now, and thank God for sharing his goodness with us.**

Close by praying that God will help the kids in your group to share with others, and thank him for the wonderful things he's shared with us. Then allow kids to eat the snacks, encouraging them to share within their groups.

Walking the Line

Friendly Focus: Real friends don't judge each other.

Scripture: Matthew 7:1-5

Overview: By attempting a task that isn't as easy as anticipated, kids will understand that they shouldn't judge others because things aren't always as they seem.

Preparation: You'll need a Bible and masking tape.

THE FUN

Place an eight- to ten-foot strip of masking tape in a line on the center of the floor. Have kids stand in a circle around the line.

Say: **I wonder if it's possible to walk along this line without stepping off. It looks pretty difficult. Do you think you could do it?**

Ask for a volunteer to attempt to "walk the line." As the volunteer comes forward, say: **One thing I forgot to tell you—before you attempt to make it across, you need to turn around and around like this.**

Carefully spin the first volunteer about ten times, then have him or her start at one end of the line and walk across to the other end. Let each student have a chance to spin around and then try to balance all the way across the line.

THE FELLOWSHIP

hen everyone has had a turn to walk the line, have kids sit in a circle. Have five volunteers read aloud one verse each from Matthew 7:1-5. Then ask:

● **What did you think when I first asked if you could "walk the line"?**

● **How did your thoughts change when I showed you why the task was so difficult? Why?**

● **What does God say will happen to us when we judge others?**

● **How did this game show us why we shouldn't judge one another?**

Say: **In our activity, we made a judgment about a task before we had all the information. In life it's easy to judge another person. But we don't have all the information. Maybe a friend isn't feeling well, is having problems at home, or has problems we can't see. Only God knows enough to judge a person.**

God tells us that instead of judging others, we should concentrate on "walking in a straight line" ourselves. If we do, we'll discover that we're so busy living God's way that we won't have time to pass judgment on our friends. Remember, real friends don't judge each other.

Close with a prayer thanking God for his love and asking for his help in not judging friends.

Be a Jonathan

Friendly Focus: Real friends stick up for each other.

Scripture: 1 Samuel 19:1-7

Overview: By participating in this interactive Bible story, kids will learn that they, too, can be like Jonathan and stick up for friends.

Preparation: You'll need a Bible, scissors, and markers. Before class, photocopy the "Just Like Jonathan" handout on page 45, and cut apart the sections. You'll need one section for every four kids. Also photocopy and sign a Jonathan Club certificate on page 46 for each child in your class.

THE FUN

ave kids sit in a circle on the floor. Open your Bible to 1 Samuel 19:1-7, and show kids the passage. Say: **I have a story to tell you. It's about three men—Saul, David, and Jonathan. You can help me tell the story.**

Whenever I say the name "Jonathan," quickly stand up and sit back down. Let's practice. Jonathan. Have kids quickly stand and sit. **Good! When I say the name "Saul," put your hands on your hips. Let's practice that. Saul.** Have kids put their hands on their hips. **And when I say "David," shake hands with a neighbor. Let's practice. David.** Have kids shake hands.

When kids are comfortable with the actions, begin the story. Pause the story after each underlined word to allow kids time to do the actions.

Say: **A powerful king named <u>Saul</u> had a son named <u>Jonathan</u> and a servant named <u>David.</u> <u>Jonathan</u> and <u>David</u> were best friends.**

<u>Jonathan</u> found out that <u>Saul</u> was planning to kill <u>David.</u> So <u>Jonathan</u> went to warn his good friend, <u>David.</u> <u>Jonathan</u> told <u>David,</u> "Go and hide. I'll find out what my father, <u>Saul,</u> is planning to do."

So <u>Jonathan</u> went to talk to <u>Saul.</u> <u>Jonathan</u> said, "You shouldn't hurt <u>David.</u> He has done nothing to you. In fact, he killed Goliath and won a great victory for our country. <u>David</u> is a good person. You shouldn't kill him."

<u>Saul</u> listened to <u>Jonathan</u> and agreed. And <u>Saul</u> promised not to kill <u>David.</u> <u>Jonathan</u> was a real friend and stuck up for <u>David.</u>

THE FELLOWSHIP

Say: **Real friends stick up for each other. Let's practice being real friends right now.** Have kids form groups of four. Give each group a section from the "Just Like Jonathan" handout (p. 45).

Say: **In your group, read the situation described in the section you just received. Then discuss and answer the questions. Each group will read its situation and present its answers to the rest of the class. You'll have five minutes to prepare. Ready? Go ahead.**

Call time after five minutes. Have each group read its situation and present its answers to the rest of the class. Encourage class members to add their perspectives to each group's discussion.

After each group has presented its situation, say: **You really had some good observations! Now that you know that real friends stick up for each other, you can officially join the Jonathan Club!**

Give each child a Jonathan Club certificate (p. 46). Hand out pens and markers, and let kids fill in their names and decorate the certificates. Then say: **Take your certificates home and display them somewhere in your room to remind you that real friends stick up for each other. Let's thank God for giving us friends.**

Close with a prayer thanking God for giving the kids real friends who will stick up for them. Ask God to help each of your kids be the kind of friend Jonathan was to David.

Sticky Buddies

Friendly Focus: Real friends stick together.

Scripture: Ruth 1:1-18

Overview: By creating their own Sticky Buddies, an edible craft, children will learn that real friends stick together.

Preparation: You'll need a Bible and scissors. For each child you'll need a long stick of gum and a round red and white peppermint candy. You'll also need a large cookie sheet to lay all of the Sticky Buddies on.

THE FUN

Have each child unwrap a stick of gum and a peppermint candy. Using scissors, have each child cut a one-inch slit down from the top edge of the gum and up from the bottom edge.

JUST LIKE JONATHAN

Situation 1

You're sitting at the lunch table at school with the really cool kids from class. You just started sitting with them this week. They start to talk about your best friend who isn't there. What they're saying isn't very nice. You're afraid that if you stick up for your friend, they'll start making fun of you, too.

What would you do?
- Keep quiet. They're just kidding around anyway.
- Tell the kids to shut up, and leave the table.
- Explain to the kids why you like your friend.

What do you think Jonathan would do in this situation?

Situation 2

Some of your friends at school decide to have a swimming party on Saturday. But the girl whose family has the pool doesn't want to invite one of your friends. You know that it would hurt your friend's feelings if she knew that you went to the party and she wasn't invited.

What would you do?
- Go to the party and hope your friend doesn't find out.
- Skip the party and do something with your friend.
- Try to convince the girl to invite your friend.

What do you think Jonathan would do in this situation?

Situation 3

You and your friend are fooling around near the teacher's desk when she is out of the room. You accidentally knock over a vase that was sitting there, and it crashes to the floor. When the teacher returns, she demands to know who did it. Your friend raises his hand, and the teacher sends him to the principal's office. Your parents have said if you get in trouble one more time at school, you can't play football.

What would you do?
- Let your friend get in trouble—it was his idea to confess.
- Tell the teacher that you were involved and risk not playing football.
- Explain to the teacher that it was an accident and say you and your friend will replace the vase.

What do you think Jonathan would do in this situation?

Jonathan Club

Official Membership Certificate

Let it be known this day that

_____
(NAME)

is now an official member of the Jonathan Club.
In recognition of your faithfulness, your loyalty, and your courage in sticking up for your friends, we welcome you to the Jonathan Club!

With affection,

_____
(TEACHER)

Jonathan Club

Official Membership Certificate

Let it be known this day that

_____
(NAME)

is now an official member of the Jonathan Club.
In recognition of your faithfulness, your loyalty, and your courage in sticking up for your friends, we welcome you to the Jonathan Club!

With affection,

_____
(TEACHER)

Buddy Builder

Try experimenting with different kinds of gum such as fruit stripe, cinnamon, strawberry, or watermelon.

Show children how to gently fold the two sections on either side of the top slit to make the arms of the Sticky Buddy. Remind students to fold carefully so as not to rip the gum.

Then demonstrate how to place the peppermint candy "head" on top of the outstretched arms. You may need to rub a small drop of water on the back of the peppermint candy to keep it stuck to the gum.

THE FELLOWSHIP

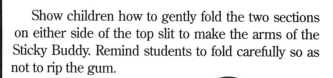

Say: **Let's stick our Sticky Buddies together on this cookie sheet, letting them touch hand to hand while we listen to a story. This Bible story is about a woman named Ruth who knew that real friends stick together.** Have kids sit together in a circle on the floor, placing the cookie sheet with the Sticky Buddies in the middle of the circle for all to see.

Open the Bible, and show children the book of Ruth. Say: **Let's all become "sticky buddies" while we're listening to the story of Ruth. Every time you hear the words "stick together," hold the hands of the kids on either side of you and give a gentle squeeze. Let go when I go on with the story.** Read the following interactive story, pausing after the words "stick together" so that children can squeeze each other's hands.

Say: **Ruth knew that real friends <u>stick together.</u>** Ruth lived with her mother-in-law, Naomi, and her sister-in-law, Orpah. They knew they had to <u>stick together</u> because they were all that was left of their little family. Their husbands had died.

One day Naomi decided to return to her homeland far away. She told Ruth and Orpah to go home to their parents. She thought they'd be better off there. Naomi kissed the women goodbye and told them to go. But Ruth and Orpah were sad. They didn't want to leave Naomi; they wanted to <u>stick together.</u> Finally Orpah left, but Ruth just couldn't let Naomi return to her homeland alone. She knew that real friends <u>stick together.</u>

Ruth said, "Naomi, where you go, I will go. Where you live, I will live. Your people will be my people, and your God will be my God." Naomi knew that she couldn't convince Ruth to go home.

Ruth and Naomi were real friends. Real friends <u>stick together.</u>

Ask:

● How do you decide who will be your best friend?

● What are some ways you can be a sticky buddy and stick together with your friends?

● When is it very important for real friends to stick together?

Say: **Real friends stick together. Let's close with a prayer while we hold the hands of our friends next to us.** Pray: **Dear God, thank you for giving us the story of Ruth. She knew that real friends stick together. Help us to be real friends who stick together. Amen.**

Let children eat their Sticky Buddies or carefully take them home.

Pepper People

Friendly Focus: Real friends don't ask you to do wrong things.

Scripture: Romans 14:13b

Overview: In this object lesson, kids will see how important it is to be a Christian example to their friends and to choose friends wisely.

Preparation: You'll need a Bible, a bowl of water, a pepper shaker, a small bar of soap, and sugar.

THE FUN

Have kids sit on the floor in a close circle around a large bowl half-filled with water.

Say: **You know, the Bible says that we have a very important job to do. We have the very important job of being Christians.** Ask:

● **How should Christians act so that others know they believe in Jesus?**

Say: **Good answers! Christians should always be loving, kind, and forgiving. But they have another important job, too.**

Open your Bible to Romans 14:13b, and show kids the passage. Then say: **Romans 14:13b says, "We must make up our minds not to do anything that will make another Christian sin."** Ask:

● **Have you ever done something wrong just to go along with your friends? How did that make you feel?**

● **How could your doing something wrong lead another Christian to sin?**

Sprinkle the pepper shaker over the water in the bowl until there is a solid layer of pepper on the water. Say: **Let's imagine that these specks of pepper are all of your friends.**

Hold up the small bar of soap. Then say: **Let's imagine that this bar of soap is you. One morning you wake up and realize that you didn't study for today's big spelling test. On the way to school, you tell your friend Carl about your problem. Carl never studies for his spelling tests. He just writes the spelling words on the palms of his hands and takes the answers from there. You know it's cheating, but Carl convinces you to take the spelling test his way. You forget that real friends don't ask you to do wrong things.**

Say: **You know that other kids in class saw you cheat.** Ask:

● **What do you think your friends are thinking about you?**

Place the bar of soap in the water. The pepper "friends" will flee to the side of the bowl.

Then say: **See, your friends are avoiding you. They thought you were their honest, Christian friend—not someone who cheats on tests.** Ask:

● **What should you do?**

Say: **You ask God to forgive you for cheating and for being a bad example. Then you go to your teacher, tell her you're sorry, and take a zero on the test.**

Sprinkle the sugar in the bowl until the pepper comes back to the middle of the water. Say: **When we're really sorry and ask God to forgive us, he does. God's forgiveness is like sweet sugar after sin leaves an ugly taste in your life.** Ask:

● **After everything you've learned, how could you help a friend in the future?**

Say: **Real friends don't ask you to do wrong things.**

THE FELLOWSHIP

After the story, ask:
- **What Christian qualities do you have that make you a good friend?**
- **When has a real friend encouraged you to do the right thing?**
- **How can surrounding yourself with Christian friends make it easier to follow God?**

Close with the following prayer: **Dear God, so many times it's easy to go along with the crowd and do things that don't show we're Christians. Help us to remember that real friends don't ask us to do wrong things. Guide us in surrounding ourselves with friends who believe in you. In Jesus' name, amen.**

Best-for-You Edible Collages

Friendly Focus: Real friends want the very best for you.

Scripture: Matthew 7:12

Overview: Kids will create their own edible collages and then "do unto others" by giving them away to friends.

Preparation: You'll need a Bible, paper plates, honey, spoons, and damp washcloths. You'll also need an assortment of "edibles" such as different-shaped cereals, M&M's, raisins, string licorice, decorating sprinkles, and chocolate chips.

THE FUN

After kids wash their hands, have them stand around a table. Give each student a paper plate. Place the assortment of snacks in the middle of the table so kids can reach them.

Say: **Let's create our own Best-for-You Edible Collages. A collage is a picture that has many parts that overlap and combine to make one beautiful picture. We're like a collage. There are many of us, and combined we make a group of people who care about each other. In our class we know that real friends want the very best for each other.**

Have each student spread one spoonful of honey on a paper plate. Then have them choose their favorite edibles to sprinkle on the honey.

Encourage kids to use their fingers as paintbrushes to create their collages.

When the collages are finished, open the Bible to the Scripture passage and say: **In the book of Matthew, it says "do to others what you want them to do to you."** Ask:

● **What do you think this passage means?**

● **What happens when you treat someone the way you'd like to be treated?**

● **Have you ever been kind to someone who then returned the favor? How did you feel?**

Say: **Let's practice what this passage says. Let's each give our edible collages, which we made just to our liking, to someone else in the room. Then let's eat!**

There may be some grumbling from kids who don't want to give up their creations. Remind kids that real friends want the very best for each other.

THE FELLOWSHIP

As kids enjoy their new edible collages, ask:

● **When is it hard to "do to others what you want them to do to you"?**

● **How can wanting the best for your friends help you become a better friend yourself?**

● **What is one thing you can do this week to show that you want the very best for your friends?**

Say: **Real friends want the very best for each other. A real friend will care when you're sad and will be full of joy when you're happy. Go out this week and treat others how you want them to treat you.**

Generous Storytelling

Friendly Focus: Real friends are generous.

Scripture: Acts 16:11-15

Overview: In this line-formation interactive story, kids will learn that Lydia was kind and generous to her friends.

Preparation: You'll need a Bible.

THE FUN

Have kids sit on the floor. Ask:

- **What does the word "generous" mean?**
- **Who do you know who is generous? Explain.**

Open your Bible to Acts 16:11-15, and show kids the passage. Say: **The Bible tells us a story, written by Luke, of a woman named Lydia who was very generous. Let's travel with Luke as we learn more about Lydia and how real friends are generous.**

Have kids stand shoulder to shoulder in the center of the room. Stand at one end of the line.

Say: **We're going to be generous and each pass the actions in this story to the person next to us in line. During the story, I'll do an action for a moment, then I'll be generous and pretend to give it to the person next to me. He or she will do the action for a moment, then pass it to the next person. We'll keep passing the actions all the way to the end of the line. Remember—real friends are generous, so keep passin' those actions!**

Tell the following story at an even pace. There will be many actions passed down the line at once—hopefully in the right order!

Begin telling the story from Acts 16:12-15. Say: **We went to the land of Philippi** (march in place), **a Roman colony and the leading city in that part of Macedonia. We stayed there for several days.** (Cross arms in front of you.)

On the Sabbath day, we went outside the city gate (open an imaginary gate) **to the river** (make wave motions with hands) **where we thought** (point to head) **we would find a special place for prayer.** (Fold hands.) **Some women had gathered there, so we sat down and talked with them.** (Open and close hands in front, as if talking.) **One of the listeners** (point to ear) **was a woman named Lydia, who sold purple cloth.** (Rub hand down arm.) **She worshiped God** (kneel and fold hands as if praying), **and he opened her mind** (point to forehead) **to pay attention to what Paul said.** (Nod in agreement.)

Then Lydia and all of the people in her house believed in Jesus. (Make cheering motions.) **She invited us to come to her home** (move arm in a welcoming motion), **and we stayed with her.** (Sit down.)

THE FELLOWSHIP

After the story, ask:

- **Why was Lydia considered a generous person?**
- **How do your friends or family members show generosity?**

● How can you be generous this week?

Say: **Real friends are generous. Lydia was generous when she invited her new friends to stay at her house. We can learn from Lydia's example and be generous to our friends, too.**

Kindness Cards V/µ4/98

Friendly Focus: Real friends are kind to each other.

Scripture: Ephesians 4:32

Overview: Kids will each create their own slightly sweet kindness cards to give to friends.

Preparation: You'll need a Bible, construction paper, markers, and tape. You'll also need a selection of each of the following wrapped treats: peppermints, chocolate kisses, and bubble gum.

THE FUN

Say: **Real friends are kind to each other. God wants us to be kind to our friends and to forgive them just as God forgives us. Let's make Kindness Cards to give to our friends.**

Set out supplies. Encourage kids to make cards by folding sheets of construction paper in half. Have each person decorate the front of a card, then tape a treat inside. Encourage kids to make up witty sayings to write inside their cards that relate to the treats taped inside. For example, kids might write sayings such as...

● "A KISS of kindness just for you!" with a chocolate kiss candy inside.

● "I MINT to tell you what a kind friend you are!" with a peppermint candy inside.

● "I'm BUBBLIN' over with pride in you!" with the bubble gum inside.

Have each student create several cards to give away to friends during the week.

THE FELLOWSHIP

hen kids have finished making their cards, have them sit on the floor. Open your Bible to Ephesians 4:32, and read the passage aloud. Then ask:

● **When was a time a friend was kind to you?**

● How can you be kind to a friend this week?

● How might giving your kindness card to a friend this week make that person feel?

Say: **Real friends are kind to each other. They care about each other's feelings and are concerned for each other. It's easy to be kind to our real friends. But God wants us to be kind and forgiving to other friends too—friends who may have hurt us and who need our forgiveness.**

Close with the following prayer: **Dear God, you are our real friend who is always kind to us. Help us follow your example, and be kind and forgiving to each other. Amen.**

Encourage kids to give the kindness cards not only to their best friends, but also to friends who may need forgiveness.

Friends Always

Friendly Focus: Real friends care for each other, even when they're apart.

Scripture: 1 Samuel 20:35-42

Overview: In this interactive story, children will learn that David and Jonathan remained friends even after they had to separate.

Preparation: You'll need Bibles.

THE FUN

Have children sit in a circle on the floor. Open your Bible to 1 Samuel 20:35-42, and show children the passage. Say: **This is a story about two best friends who cared about each other even when they were apart. I'll need your help telling the story. As I tell you the story, do what I do.**

Read aloud the following story, and demonstrate the actions. Be sure to read slowly so children have time to copy your motions. (Older kids might enjoy acting out the story in an exaggerated pantomime.)

Once there was a boy named David	*(Hold up the index finger of your left hand.)*
And a boy named Jonathan.	*(Hold up the index finger of your right hand.)*
They were best friends.	*(Put your two index fingers side by side.)*

One day Jonathan found out that David was in danger.	*(Put your right hand to your right ear.)*
The king didn't like David and wanted to hurt him.	*(Put hands on hips.)*
So Jonathan ran to David and told him to hurry and hide.	*(Bounce your two index fingers side by side, as if running.)*
When David found out he had to leave, he was sad.	*(Bend your left index finger.)*
Jonathan was sad too.	*(Bend your right index finger.)*
David and Jonathan cried.	*(Put your index fingers to your eyes as if wiping away tears.)*
They hugged each other.	*(Curl your index fingers around each other.)*
Jonathan said, "I'll miss you, but we'll always be friends."	*(Hold your right hand in front of you as if preparing to shake hands.)*
David said, "God will help us care for each other even when we're apart."	*(Grasp your right hand with your left hand.)*

THE FELLOWSHIP

After the story, ask:

- How do you think Jonathan felt when he found out David, his best friend, was in danger?
- Have you ever had to move away or leave a good friend? How did you feel? Do you still care for your friend?
- How can you show your friends that you care for them when you're apart?

Say: Sometimes we forget about friends when we're not with them. But God wants us to care for our friends and show love to them even when they're not with us. Real friends care for each other—even when they're apart.

Friendship Foundation

Friendly Focus: Real friends don't gossip about each other.

Scripture: Proverbs 17:9

Overview: In this fun skit, children will learn that gossip undermines the foundations of friendship.

Preparation: You'll need a Bible.

THE FUN

xplain to children that they will be participating in an improvisational skit. If they're nervous about participating in a skit, explain to them that this skit will not involve any talking—just actions.

Assign each student one of the following roles:

- Friends (two children)
- House (two to eight children)
- Door
- Sun
- Trees (as many kids as necessary)
- Winds (as many kids as necessary)

Direct kids to act out their roles as they're mentioned in the story.

Read the following script, pausing to let kids act out the italicized directions.

Once there were two friends who set out to build a house.

(Two Friends smile and wave at each other.)

They laid a solid foundation, built four straight walls, and put in a strong door.

(Two Friends pretend to lay a foundation. House actors stand next to each other to form walls, and hold arms overhead to form a peak. Door stands at the front of House.)

The sun came out and smiled on the house.

(Sun forms a circle with arms and stands near House.)

The trees grew outside in the lovely yard.

(Trees stand around House, holding arms out at sides.)

The friends loved their new house and took care of it.

(Two Friends pat House and smile.)

One day, though, some strong winds began to blow on the house.

(Winds run in and blow on House.)

The winds blew harder and harder.

(Winds run around House, blow on House, and wave arms.)

The walls shook.

(House shakes.)

The door swayed.

(Door sways.)

Finally, the foundation of the house gave way, and the house collapsed.

(House and Door fall to ground.)

Love forgets mistakes; nagging about them parts the best of friends.

THE FELLOWSHIP

After the skit, have kids give themselves a big round of applause. Then form a circle. Ask:

● **How was the house in this story like a friendship that two friends might build?**

● **What kinds of things can hurt or destroy a friendship?**

Read aloud Proverbs 17:9. Say: **According to this verse, gossip can destroy a friendship just as the strong winds destroyed the house in our skit. Just as the house needed a strong foundation to support it, a friendship needs a strong foundation of trust to keep it from falling apart.** Ask:

● **What does gossip do to trust in a friendship? Why?**

● **Have you ever seen gossip destroy a friendship? What happened?**

● **How can you protect your friendships from gossip?**

Say: **God wants us to show love to our friends by refusing to talk about them behind their backs. He also wants us to help others by not listening to gossip. Remember, real friends don't gossip about each other.**

Walking in My Shoes

Friendly Focus: Real friends care about each other's feelings.

Scripture: Mark 14:32-42

Overview: In this creative role-play, kids will learn to have empathy for one another.

Preparation: You'll need Bibles, scissors, and photocopies of the "Friend or Foe?" handout on page 60. Before class, cut apart the scenarios from the handout. You'll need one scenario for each pair of students. It's OK if more than one pair use the same scenario.

THE FUN

Form pairs. Give each pair one of the scenarios from the handout. Tell partners they need to decide who will play each role. Explain to pairs that they'll each have five minutes to read their scenarios and create a script to act out for the rest of the class. Also tell kids that during their performances, you'll be calling "freeze." When you say "freeze," actors should switch roles.

After five minutes, gather kids together. Have pairs take turns acting out their scenarios. Call "freeze" during each scene, and have partners switch roles.

Lead the "audience" in applause after each pair's presentation.

Buddy Builder

You may want to provide simple props and costumes to add to the fun!

THE FELLOWSHIP

After each performance, ask the following questions.

Ask the actors:

● **How did you feel about your partner's character at the beginning of your presentation?**

● **How did your feelings change when you switched roles with your partner?**

Then ask the class:

● **How could these two friends have cared about each other's feelings better?**

After all pairs have presented their scenarios, say: **There's an old saying, "You can't really know a person until you've walked a mile in their shoes." In this activity, we switched roles to see what it was like in our partners' shoes. Trying to imagine what our friends are going through is one way to understand their feelings better. But that's not always easy to do. Even Jesus' friends had trouble. I'll show you what I mean.**

Give each pair a Bible. Have partners take turns reading to each other the verses in Mark 14:32-42.

Say: **In this passage, we see Jesus going through a tough time. His friends don't seem to care about his feelings.** Ask:

● **What could Jesus' disciples have done to understand his feelings better?**

● **How could they have shown Jesus that they cared about his feelings?**

● **How can you show your friends that you care about their feelings?**

Say: **Real friends care about each other's feelings. Let's ask God to help us be real friends who care about each other's feelings. As we pray, think of a person you'd like to understand and care about better. This could be someone at school, a parent, a teacher, or even your brother or sister.**

Pray: **Dear God, thank you for always caring about our feelings. Please help us to understand and care about our friends'** feelings. And help us to show our friends that we love them, just as you show your love for us. In Jesus' name, amen.

A Big Hand for You!

Friendly Focus: Real friends appreciate each other.

Scripture: 2 Timothy 1:1-6

Overview: Kids will affirm each other as they learn the importance of expressing appreciation to their friends.

Preparation: You'll need Bibles, scissors, construction paper, and markers.

THE FUN

As kids arrive, give each one a sheet of construction paper, scissors, and a marker. Tell each person to trace one hand onto the construction paper, cut around the outline, then write his or her name on one side of the paper hand.

Gather kids in a circle. Say: **We're going to show how much we appreciate each other. We'll pass our paper hands around the circle to the left. Each time you receive a paper hand, write on the hand one thing you like about the person it belongs to. Try to think of inner qualities rather than outer qualities to write about. For example, instead of writing, "I really like your hair," you might write, "I like how you're always so nice." We'll keep**

FRIEND OR FOE?

Characters: Two friends

What's Happening: These two friends used to be together all the time. But lately, Friend #1 has been eating lunch and playing with a new kid in class. Friend #2 feels jealous and lonely.

Characters: Two friends

What's Happening: Friend #1 is upset because his parents are getting a divorce. The divorce is all Friend #1 talks about. Friend #2 is getting tired of hearing about it.

Characters: Two friends

What's Happening: Friend #1 heard that Friend #2 has been spreading nasty rumors about her (or him). Friend #1 is hurt and has stopped talking to Friend #2. Friend #2 doesn't understand why Friend #1 is acting so cold.

Characters: Two friends

What's Happening: One friend is upset because he (or she) got in a big fight with his (or her) parents. The other friend doesn't understand why that's such a big deal. The second friend would rather talk about the birthday party they're both going to on Saturday.

passing the paper hands around the circle until they come back to their original owners. Ready? Pass your paper hand to the person on your left! Have kids pass the paper hands around the circle until the hands come back to their owners.

THE FELLOWSHIP

sk kids to form trios. Give each trio a Bible, and have one child in each trio read aloud 2 Timothy 1:1-6. Then have kids discuss the following questions in their trios. Ask:

● **What did Paul appreciate about his friend Timothy?**

● **How do you think Timothy felt when Paul told him he appreciated him?**

● **How did you feel when you read the appreciation notes your friends wrote?**

● **How can you show appreciation to your friends this week?**

Say: **Real friends appreciate each other. Let's ask God to help us always appreciate our friends.** Pray: **Dear God, thank you for giving us friends. Help us to always show our friends how much we appreciate them. In Jesus' name, amen.** Have kids take their paper hands home to remind them to appreciate their friends.

Mirror Me!

Friendly Focus: Real friends are good examples for each other.

Scripture: 1 Timothy 4:11-12

Overview: By physically "mirroring" each other's actions, kids will understand what it means to act as examples to others.

Preparation: You'll need Bibles.

THE FUN

sk kids to form pairs. Have kids in each pair choose who will be the Example and who will be the Follower. Have partners stand toe to toe, facing each other. Say: **If you're the Example, it's your job to make motions and facial expressions for the Follower to follow. Remember, this isn't a competition, so you'll need to keep your motions slow and simple enough for your partner to follow. Followers, it's your job to try to mirror everything the Examples do.**

Have kids play for a minute or two, then have them switch roles.

✴THE FELLOWSHIP

Have kids stay in their pairs, and give each pair a Bible. Have kids read 1 Timothy 4:11-12 in their pairs.

Then have kids form a circle. Ask:

● **Was it easier to be the Example or the Follower in our activity? Why?**

● **Is it easier to be an Example or a Follower in real life? Explain.**

● **What did Paul tell Timothy about being a good example?**

● **How can you be a good example to your friends?**

Say: **Real friends are good examples for each other. Let's ask God to help us be the kind of good examples our friends will want to follow.** Pray: **Dear God, please help us be good examples for our friends. Thank you for sending Jesus as our perfect example. Amen.**

Respectfully Yours

Friendly Focus: Real friends treat each other with respect.

Scripture: James 2:1-4

Overview: By wearing labels, kids will learn what it means to respect each other, regardless of their differences.

Preparation: You'll need Bibles, paper, a marker, and tape. Before class, use slips of paper to make one label for each student. Write one of the following statements on each label:

● I'm wearing brand name clothing. Treat me with respect.

- My clothes are old and faded. Reject me.
- I tell funny jokes, and I make people laugh. Treat me with respect.
- I'm kind of quiet and shy, and I feel awkward sometimes. Reject me.
- I get good grades, but I've been labeled "Teacher's Pet." Reject me.
- My grades in school are average, but I'm the fastest runner in my class. Treat me with respect.

THE FUN

As kids arrive, tape one of the labels on each of their backs. Say: **As I'm tapping these labels on your backs, you can read each other's labels silently. But don't tell anyone what his or her label says.**

After each child has a label, say: **When I say "mingle," walk around the room and greet each other. Read the label on each person's back, and treat him or her according to what the label says. For** example, **if someone's label says, "I'm wearing brand name clothing. Treat me with respect," you might smile at that person, shake his or her hand, or pat the person on the shoulder. Ready? Mingle!**

Buddy Builder

Be sensitive to kids who may actually be thought of in ways similar to your labels. Try to give kids labels that they don't experience in real life.

THE FELLOWSHIP

Let kids mingle for about two minutes, then have them form pairs. Ask kids to remove and read their labels. Then give each pair a Bible. Have pairs read James 2:1-4 together.

Say: **According to this passage, being a friend means treating others with respect, no matter what.** Have kids answer the following questions in their pairs. Invite pairs to share their insights with the rest of the class. Ask:

- **How did it feel to be respected when you were mingling? rejected?** Allow several kids a chance to answer.
- **What does it mean to treat others with respect?**
- **How can we show respect for others even if they're different from us?**

Say: **Real friends treat each other with respect. Let's ask God to help us show others respect.** Lead kids in prayer.

Those Who Can, Teach!

Friendly Focus: Real friends teach each other what's right.

Scripture: Acts 18:24-28

Overview: By teaching each other simple actions, kids will learn what it means to teach each other what's right.

Preparation: Set out Bibles, plain paper, and pencils for kids to use. Before class, make photocopies of the "Teacher Time" handout on page 65. Cut apart the sections of the handouts. You'll need one section for each student.

THE FUN

Have kids form pairs. Give each student a section from the handout, making sure that partners don't have the same section. Say: **Your job today is to teach your partner what is printed on the paper I've given you. In your pair, decide who will be the Teacher and who will be the Student. After two minutes, I'll call time so you can switch roles. When you're the Student, do exactly what your Teacher tells you to do. Use these supplies if you need them.** Call time after two minutes, and remind kids to switch roles. Circulate around the room to offer help as needed.

THE FELLOWSHIP

After each person has had a chance to be the Teacher, ask:
- **What was it like to be the Teacher in this activity? the Student?**
- **What's the hardest part about trying to teach someone?**
- **What's the hardest part when you're trying to learn something new?**

Say: **Let's look at two people in the Bible who were good teachers.** Read aloud Acts 18:24-28.

Say: **Real friends teach each other what's right. In this Bible passage we see Priscilla and Aquila teaching their friend Apollos about God.** Ask:
- **How did Priscilla and Aquila go about teaching Apollos?**
- **How did their teaching help Apollos?**
- **How can we teach our friends what is right?**

Say: **Priscilla and Aquila wanted to teach Apollos the truth about God and Jesus. They helped him understand more about Jesus so he could teach others. Real friends teach each other what's right.**

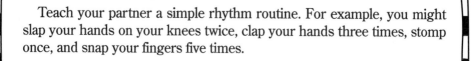

TEACHER TIME

Teach your partner a simple rhythm routine. For example, you might slap your hands on your knees twice, clap your hands three times, stomp once, and snap your fingers five times.

Teach your partner how to make a paper airplane, a paper hat, or a paper boat. If you don't know how, just do the best you can.

Teach your partner your favorite Bible verse. Help him or her to memorize it.

Teach your partner the directions to your house. Have your partner draw a map to make sure he or she remembers.

Which Way's the Right Way?

Friendly Focus: Real friends don't think they're better than others.

Scripture: Romans 12:16

Overview: By role playing the best and worst ways to handle situations, kids will learn to treat others with equality.

Preparation: You'll need Bibles, index cards, and a marker. Before class, write one of the following scenarios on each index card. You'll need one card for every four or five students.

● "Best Way: Your group of friends sees a new person sitting alone during lunch."

● "Worst Way: Your group of friends sees a new person sitting alone during lunch."

● "Best Way: One of the students in your math class aced a really hard test, and the rest of the class did very poorly."

● "Worst Way: One of the students in your math class aced a really hard test, and the rest of the class did very poorly."

THE FUN

Have kids form groups of four or five. Give each group an index card with a scenario written on it. Tell groups that they'll have five minutes to create short skits showing the best or worst ways to handle the situations on their cards. Tell kids that each person in the group must have a part in the skit. As kids work, offer help to any groups that may need ideas.

After five minutes, have groups take turns performing their skits for the entire class. Lead the class in a round of applause after each skit.

Buddy Builder

If you have an uneven number of groups, be sure to have the class discuss an alternate way of handling the situation that was presented by only one group.

THE FELLOWSHIP

After kids have performed their skits, have groups discuss the following questions. Allow volunteers to share their insights with the rest of the class. Ask:

● **How did you feel about the situation your group acted out?**

● **How were your actions in your skit like how you should or** shouldn't treat others in real life?

Give each group a Bible. Have one child from each group read aloud Romans 12:16. Ask:

● **What does this verse say about how real friends should treat each other?**

● **How can this verse help you treat your friends fairly?**

Say: **Real friends don't think they're better than others. If you're tempted this week to think you're better than your friends, remember what this verse has to say.**

Show Me the Way!

Friendly Focus: Real friends help you even when you make mistakes.

Scripture: Ecclesiastes 4:10

Overview: By helping each other through a simple obstacle course, children will understand how helpful friends can be.

Preparation: You'll need a Bible and one blindfold for every two children. You'll also need to set up a simple obstacle course using available classroom items. For example, you might have children crawl under a table, walk around a chair, and walk backward to the finish line.

THE FUN

Let children form pairs, and give each pair a blindfold. Have children in each pair decide who will wear the blindfold first and who will be the Helper. Assist the Helper in each pair to tie the blindfold around his or her partner's head. Take the Helpers aside, and show the obstacle course to them, explaining that they'll be guiding their partners through the course.

Bring the whole group back together, and say: **Helpers, your job is to get your partners safely through the obstacle course. But you can't touch your partners. Remember that your partners are trusting you, so be sure to give them good instructions.** Have pairs proceed through the obstacle course one pair at a time. After partners finish, have them trade places and complete the course again.

THE FELLOWSHIP

After pairs complete the course, have kids form a circle. Ask:

● **What was it like to help your partners when they were blindfolded?**

- How did it feel to be helped when you couldn't see?
- What would it have been like to have gone through this course without someone to help you?

Read aloud Ecclesiastes 4:10. Then ask:

- What does this verse say about helping others?
- How was helping your partner in this activity like helping someone in real life, even when that person made mistakes?
- When have you helped someone even when that person made mistakes?
- When has someone helped you even though you made mistakes?

Say: **Real friends help you even when you make mistakes.** Ask:

- What can you do this week to help someone else?

Say: **Let's pray together.** Pray: **Thank you, God, for giving us friends to help us even when we make mistakes. Help us to be good friends, too. In Jesus' name, amen.**

2/11/98 **From the Heart**

Lola

Friendly Focus: Real friends pray for each other.

Scripture: Acts 12:5-18

Overview: By exchanging names during a Bible story game, each child will have someone to pray for.

Preparation: You'll need a Bible, new or used envelopes, markers or crayons, slips of paper, and scissors. Before class, make one photocopy of the "Have a Heart" pattern on page 70. Then trace the pattern onto the lower corners of business envelopes. Each student will need a Heart-Pocket Envelope. Refer to the picture on the pattern for directions.

THE FUN

Give each child an envelope. If time permits, have kids cut the heart shapes along the dotted lines on their envelopes. Otherwise, do this step for children before they arrive.

Encourage children to decorate their hearts with markers or crayons. Then give students paper slips, and have them write their names on the slips. Explain that the paper slips should be folded and tucked inside the heart pockets on their envelopes.

THE FELLOWSHIP

Have children sit in a circle on the floor with their Heart-Pocket Envelopes.

Say: **Real friends pray for each other, especially in times of trouble. We're going to hear a story from the Bible about a man named Peter, one of Jesus' disciples. In this story, Peter was in BIG trouble—he was in prison! King Herod didn't like Christians, so he ordered that they be arrested and sent to prison.**

But while Peter was in prison, his friends prayed for him. Then God sent an angel to rescue Peter! As I read the story out loud, we'll pass our hearts around the circle. Every time I say the name "Peter," give your heart to the person on your right. When you hear me say "angel," give your heart to the person on your left. We'll continue to pass hearts from person to person until the story is over.

Read aloud Acts 12:5-18. Pause slightly after the words "Peter" and "angel" to give kids time to pass their hearts to the left or to the right. When you finish reading the Bible story, tell kids to hold onto the hearts they ended up with but not to read the names inside yet. Ask:

- **How do you think Peter felt when he had to go to prison?**
- **How do you think Peter's friends felt?**
- **How did the prayers of Peter's friends help him?**
- **How can our prayers help our friends?**

Say: **Peter's friends didn't give up on him or forget him. They knew Peter's best protection would come from God, so they prayed to God and asked him to protect and comfort Peter.**

Let each child look inside the Heart-Pocket Envelope to see whose name is tucked inside.

Say: **When you pray for your friends this week, remember to pray for this friend from church, too. Keep the heart with you during the week, or put it near your bed at night as a reminder to pray for the person whose name you received. Remember, real friends pray for each other.**

Matchless Pairs

Friendly Focus: Real friends help each other.

Scripture: Acts 18:1-4, 18-26

HAVE A HEART

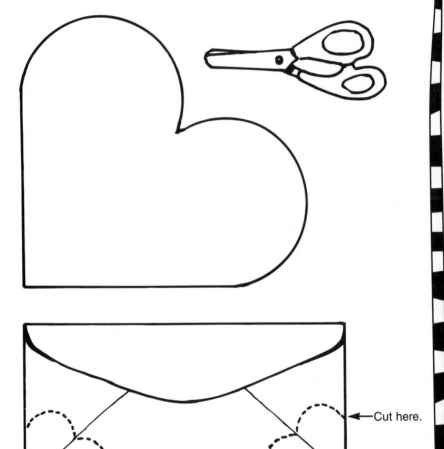

←Cut here.

←Do not
cut here.

Overview: Children will collect specific colors of M&M's as they meet and greet fellow "hunters."

Preparation: You'll need Bibles, a bag of M&M's, and plastic sandwich bags. Before class, place fifteen M&M's in each plastic bag. You'll need to prepare a bag for each pair of children.

THE FUN

ave children find partners, and distribute a bag of M&M's to each pair. Say: **Let's play a friendly game to see how well you and your partner can help each other. The object of this game is to trade your M&M's with other pairs of kids until you have all one color of candy in your bag. You may trade only one candy at a time, so you may have to go back to the same partners if they have a color you need. We'll continue until each pair of friends has only one color of candy in their bags.**

THE FELLOWSHIP

hen each pair has only one color of candy in their bag, stop the game and ask:

● **What was it like trying to collect one color of candy?**
● **How did helping your friends make it easier to accomplish this challenge?**

Say: **Helping each other isn't just fun, it's what God wants us to do. Let's read about some friends who helped Paul tell others about Jesus.** Read aloud Acts 18:1-4, 18-26. Then ask:

● **How did Aquila and Priscilla help Paul?**
● **In what ways did Paul help his friends?**
● **Why is it important for friends to help one another?**
● **How can you help your friends this week?**

Say: **This game was a fun example of friends helping one another. We all needed something that someone else had, and we all helped each other get one color of candy in each bag.**

And do you know what the sweetest part of this game was? We had fun with friends! Now let's close by turning in our bags of candy and getting fresh candy to nibble.

Listen Up!

Friendly Focus: Real friends listen to each other.

Scripture: James 1:19

Overview: Children will discover interesting facts about their friends by being good listeners.

Preparation: You'll need a Bible, scissors, tape, a marker, and colored construction paper. Before class, cut out a large construction paper heart, star, circle, and triangle. Tape one large shape to each wall of the room. Then cut out a small construction paper heart for each child.

THE FUN

ecretly hand each child a paper heart, and tell him or her to keep the shape hidden until asked to reveal it. Help children find partners. Then say: **Look at the shapes on the wall. What shapes do you see?** Allow children to identify the shapes and their locations on the wall.

Then say: **I've handed each of you a shape to keep hidden. Let's pretend you are the shape I just handed you. The object of this game is to ask each other yes-or-no questions to see which shape you are. You might ask questions such as "Do you have five points?" or "Do you have rounded sides?" Ask your questions carefully and listen to your partner's answers. Then when you think you know what shape your partner is, go sit under that shape on the wall.**

THE FELLOWSHIP

hen everyone is sitting under the paper heart on the wall, say: **You were pretty good detectives!** Ask:

● **How did asking the right questions help you determine your partner's identity?**

● **In what ways did listening help?**

● **How can listening help you become a good friend?**

Say: **Too often, friends are quick to talk but slow to listen. We may think we know a friend, but we may not really understand how that person thinks or feels, or even what makes our friend happy or sad. To really know someone, you have to be a good listener. Let's listen to what the Bible says about listening.** Read aloud James 1:19. Then ask:

● **Why is it better to listen than to speak?**

● How can you be a better listener?

Say: **You probably were surprised to discover that everyone was a heart-shape in our game. I did that on purpose. The hearts are meant to remind us that listening is a good way to show friends we care. Real friends listen to each other. Take your paper heart home and tape it in a place you'll see often. Each time you look at your paper heart, think of a friend you can help by being a good listener.**

Actions Speak Louder Than Words

Friendly Focus: Real friends love each other.

Scripture: Colossians 3:12-14

Overview: Kids will learn that loving actions are even more important than words.

Preparation: You'll need Bibles, paper, a paper sack, markers, and index cards. Before class, write one of the following words or phrases on each index card: "Hug," "Pat on the shoulder," "Pat on the back," "Hold hands," "Smile," "Frown," "Growl," and "Shove (gently)." Place the cards in a paper sack. Write the words "Loving Actions" on one sheet of paper, and the words "Crabby Actions" on another sheet of paper. Tape the paper signs to opposite walls of the room.

THE FUN

Have kids find partners, and gather in the center of the room. If you have more than sixteen kids, form trios or small groups. Let each pair choose a card from the paper sack. Ask kids to keep the words on their cards a secret.

Say: **Let's play a fun game of charades. You and your partner will have an opportunity to act out the words on your card. Some of you have "loving action" cards and some of you have "crabby action" cards. After you've acted out the words on your card, the rest of us will hop to the paper on the wall that describes your action.** Point out the Loving Actions and Crabby Actions signs.

Begin the game. After each pair has acted out the words on their card, have all the kids hop to the appropriate sign on the wall. Then have them return to the center of the room. Continue until all the cards have been acted out.

THE FELLOWSHIP

Gather kids under the Loving Action sign. Ask:

- **Which of the actions we did would make a person feel accepted and loved? Why?**
- **Do our actions always match what we say? Explain.**
- **What does the saying "actions speak louder than words" mean?**
- **Why is it important to show a friend love instead of just saying the words?**

Say: **It's often easy to say we love someone, but it may not be so easy to show our love. Let's read what the Bible says about loving each other.** Have a volunteer read aloud Colossians 3:12-14. Then ask:

- **What loving actions are we supposed to show our friends?**
- **How can those actions express our love better than words?**

Say: **God wants us to tell others we love them. But he also says a loving friend will show love in ways such as forgiveness, acceptance, kindness, gentleness, and mercy.**

It's important to remember that what we say is heard—and what we do is seen and felt. Actions do speak louder than words! Show your partner you care by giving him or her a high five.

The Comfort Puzzle

Friendly Focus: Real friends comfort you when you're afraid.

Scripture: Matthew 8:23-27

Overview: Children will discover ways to help calm their friends' fears.

Preparation: You'll need a Bible and several jigsaw puzzles containing large pieces. Preschool puzzles work well for this activity. If you can't find puzzles, simply glue magazine pictures to poster board, then cut out two puzzle pieces for each child, plus a couple for you, and one extra piece. The puzzle pieces must easily fit together.

THE FUN

Gather children in a circle. If your group is very large, have kids form several smaller circles. Hand each child two puzzle pieces and take a couple for yourself. Hold back one puzzle piece. If there are extra pieces, place them in the center of the circle and fit them in as you go.

Say: **Everyone is afraid of something. You might be afraid of loud thunder or of snakes. Or you might have a friend who's afraid of the dark. But sometimes knowing how to comfort a friend who's scared is like a puzzle—we don't know what piece to offer.**

Let's go around the circle and tell one thing we're afraid of or that we used to be afraid of. Then place your puzzle piece in the center of the circle. When we're done, we'll go around the circle one more time and tell something that helps us when we're afraid. I'll start.

Name something you're afraid of, then place your puzzle piece in the center. Fit together puzzle pieces as each child names his or her fear. Continue until everyone has had a chance to place a puzzle piece in the center. Then go around the circle again, and have children name things that comfort them when they're afraid. Be sure all but one puzzle piece is in place when they're finished.

THE FELLOWSHIP

Ask:

- **How can fears stop us from being close to God? our friends? our families?**
- **How can you comfort a friend when he or she is afraid?**

Say: **Being afraid isn't any fun, but friends can do a lot to comfort and help each other. Let's read about a time Jesus' friends were afraid and how he comforted them.** Read aloud Matthew 8:23-27. Then ask:

- **How did Jesus comfort his friends?**
- **In what ways can we comfort our friends?**

Hold up the missing puzzle piece and say: **We've named a lot of good ways to comfort and help our friends when they're afraid. But the best way to complete the comfort puzzle is to comfort our friends with Jesus' love!** Fit the remaining puzzle piece into the puzzle. **Jesus' love comforts anyone, any time. The next time your friend is afraid, be ready to comfort him or her with Jesus!**

Big Birthday Bash

Friendly Focus: Real friends rejoice in each other.

Scripture: Philippians 1:3-11

Overview: Children will rejoice with friends and share their happiest memories.

Preparation: You'll need a Bible, birthday candles, plain cupcakes, canned icing, and plastic knives. Also provide a variety of decorating goodies such as candy sprinkles, raisins, and peanuts.

THE FUN

et out the cupcakes, canned icing, plastic knives, and decorating goodies. Gather children in the center of the room and hand each child a birthday candle.

Say: **Aren't birthdays wonderful? They're happy celebrations of who we are and what we're becoming. One of the best things about birthdays is sharing them with our friends.**

Let's have a big birthday bash where we can all tell our happy birthday memories. We'll go around the circle. When it's your turn, hold your candle high and tell one of your best birthday memories. Then we'll all clap and say, "Happy birthday to you!"

Continue until everyone has had a turn to tell a special memory.

THE FELLOWSHIP

ay: **That was fun! And it doesn't matter whether today is your birthday or not. We can always rejoice in how special our friends really are.** Ask:

● **Why is it fun to recognize how special our friends are?**

● **How can sharing happy memories bring us closer to our friends?**

Read aloud Philippians 1:3-11. Then ask:

● **Why did Paul rejoice in his friends?**

● **How can you be happy and rejoice in your friends every day?**

Say: **Let's end our birthday bash by making more happy memories with friends. Find one or two partners and come decorate special birthday cakes to nibble and enjoy together.** Following the "birthday party," invite children to keep their birthday candles as reminders of rejoicing in their friends.

Hot Spot

Friendly Focus: Real friends share their faith.

Scripture: Matthew 28:19-20

Overview: In this exciting game, kids will travel around the room and learn ways to share their faith with friends.

Preparation: You'll need a Bible, paper plates, tape, and markers. Before class, write one of each of the following situations on a paper plate. If your class is very large, make two sets of plates.

- Your friend has a sick grandma.
- Your friend is worried about a test.
- Your friend is angry at his sister for breaking a new toy.
- Your friend doesn't believe God can make miracles happen.
- Your friend is afraid of going to the dentist.
- Your friend doesn't know that prayer helps.

Tape the paper plates to the floor in rows, interspersing plain paper plates with the plates that are written on. Leave about two feet of space between each plate and row.

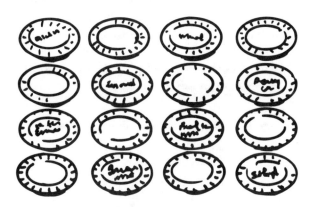

THE FUN

ave each child stand on a paper plate or "spot." Say: **Sometimes our friends find themselves in tough situations. They may be afraid of something, or worried, or sick, or just unsure of what's going on in their lives. It's during those tough times that we have a chance to share our faith and God's love with them. There are lots of spots on the floor—and some of them have tough-time situations written on them.**

I'll give you a traveling direction such as "Move one spot to your left" or "Move two spots forward." Follow the directions, then read the situation you're standing on. Turn to one of your "neighbors" and share your faith by explaining how God could help in that situation. If you're standing on a blank spot, you can be a listener. If I call, "Hot spot!" go stand on a spot you haven't visited yet. Then share your faith with one of your neighbors.

If someone can't move forward or backward, have that person go to the first or last spot of that row. Continue until you've given at least five traveling directions and each child has had at least two chances to share his or her faith with someone.

THE FELLOWSHIP

When children have finished playing, have everyone sit on a spot. Ask:

● **What did you learn about your own faith as we played this game?**

● **How can sharing your faith help friends?**

● **How does sharing your faith bring you closer to your friends? closer to God?**

Say: **Let's read what Jesus said about sharing faith with others.** Have a volunteer read aloud Matthew 28:19-20. Then ask:

● **Should we share our faith just with friends? Explain.**

● **Why do you think sharing our faith is so important to Jesus?**

Say: **Friends can share a lot, but sharing faith is the best thing we can share. In fact, friends and faith go together hand in hand. Real friends share their faith, and that can help us grow closer to God!**

Potato Pals

Friendly Focus: Real friends honor each other.

Scripture: Romans 12:10

Overview: Kids will sculpt fun potatoes and affirm friends.

Preparation: You'll need a Bible, toothpicks, colored paper, a paper sack, tape, and colored markers. You'll also need a raw potato for each child. Write each child's name on a small slip of paper, and place the paper slips in a sack.

Invite each child to draw the name of a friend out of the sack and to keep the name secret. Say: **Honoring our friends means we treat them with respect and kindness. It means we genuinely enjoy our friends and want to do special things for them.**

Today we'll make Potato Pals that honor the secret friends whose names we drew. For example, putting a big paper smile on the potato would show how friendly you think your secret friend is. Or adding a bouquet of paper flowers shows how nice you consider that person. Remember, the Potato Pal you make should honor your secret friend and show respect and kindness. When we're finished, we'll present the Potato Pals to our secret friends.

Give each child a potato, toothpicks, and colored paper scraps. Have kids make features and accompaniments with their paper scraps, and use toothpicks to attach the paper scraps to their potatoes. Allow time for all the kids to finish decorating their potatoes.

THE FELLOWSHIP

Gather kids in a group, and have them hold their Potato Pals. Ask:
● **Was it easy or hard to show how you honor your secret friend? Explain.**

● **How does honoring someone help you know them better? appreciate them more?**

Say: **We know that being kind and giving to friends is important. But we often overlook giving our friends honor. Let's see what the Bible says about honoring our friends.** Read aloud Romans 12:10. Then ask:

● In what ways can we honor our friends?

● How does giving honor to friends make us less selfish? more thoughtful?

Say: **Your Potato Pals look wonderful! Let's take turns holding them up. When it's your turn, hold your Potato Pal high and describe positive things about your secret friend. Then we'll guess who your secret friend is. Afterward, you can present your Potato Pal to your friend to take home.** Continue until all the secret friends have been identified and honored.

Circle of Love

Friendly Focus: Real friends put others before themselves.

Scripture: Romans 15:1-2

Overview: Kids will find out how acting in unselfish ways can accomplish seemingly impossible tasks.

Preparation: You'll need a Bible and masking tape. Before this activity, use the masking tape to outline a twelve-inch circle on the floor.

THE FUN

Gather kids near the masking tape circle. Say: **I have a challenge for you. Do you see that small masking tape circle on the floor? When I say "go," everyone must fit his or her feet in that circle. Ready? Go!** Be prepared for some scurrying and perhaps a little selfish shoving as all the kids try to fit their feet in the circle. It's doubtful whether your kids can accomplish this task!

Call time after a few seconds.

THE FELLOWSHIP

Have kids sit around the circle. Ask:

● **Why do you think it was difficult for everyone to fit inside the circle?**

● **How was this activity like the way we selfishly act sometimes?**

● **What might have happened if you had calmly invited another person to go ahead of you?**

Say: **Sometimes we forget that God wants us to be giving. We end up acting in selfish ways and may hurt our friends in the** process. **Look at what the Bible tells us about putting others before us.** Have a volunteer read aloud Romans 15:1-2. Then ask:

● **Why is putting our friends before us a good way to show we care?**

● **In what ways can you act less selfishly to your friends this week?**

Say: **Now that you've learned about putting your friends before you, let's try our circle trick again. This time, offer to let someone else put his or her feet in first—and try piling feet on top of feet instead of pushing others aside. I'll give you a hint: You may have to sit down to accomplish this!**

Allow kids time to calmly fit all their feet in the circle—it can be done! Then say: **Putting friends before yourself is one way to show kindness and love. And just like a never-ending circle, the circle of giving keeps going 'round and 'round!**

Take Care!

Friendly Focus: Real friends take care of each other.

Scripture: Ruth 2:4-23

Overview: In this fast-paced relay, kids will discover how and why friends take care for each other.

Preparation: You'll need a Bible, several blankets, paper cups, plastic spoons, and cereal loops. Before this activity, pour about one-fourth cup of cereal into each paper cup. Prepare a cup for each student.

THE FUN

lace the plastic spoons, blankets, and paper cups containing the cereal loops at one end of the room. Have kids form groups of four. Say: **This is a fun kind of relay game. In your group, you'll need to choose one person to be the Sickster and three to be the Caretakers. The Sicksters have bad colds. They need tender loving care from the Caretakers.**

When I say "go," the Sicksters in each group will sit or lie down on the floor. The Caretakers in each group must rush to the other end of the room. One Caretaker can get a blanket to cover the Sickster. One Caretaker can get the cup of cereal, and

one Caretaker can bring the plastic spoon. When you've covered the Sickster and helped him or her eat a spoonful of cereal, sit down and raise your hands. Ready? Go!

After the first group is finished, rotate roles and continue playing until each child has been the Sickster. Use a fresh plastic spoon for each child.

THE FELLOWSHIP

When the relays are finished, ask:
- When was a time you took care of a friend?
- How did taking care of that person help you become better friends?

Say: We all need tender loving care once in a while. Maybe it's because we're feeling sick. Or because we had a bad day at school. Or because our feelings were hurt. Nothing feels as good as being cared for by a friend! Here's what the Bible says about taking care of each other. Read aloud Ruth 2:4-23. Then ask:
- In what ways did Ruth care for Naomi?
- How did taking care of Naomi bring Ruth closer to her friend? closer to God?
- How can taking care of your friends help bring you nearer to God?

Say: Real friends take care of each other. Taking care of your friends is another way of saying, "I love you—you're special and you're worth it!" It's important to realize that when we take care of friends, we're sharing God's love!

Strong Structures

Friendly Focus: Real friends support you when you need help.

Scripture: Luke 10:25-37

Overview: In this building activity, kids will learn how important support can be.

Preparation: You'll need Bibles, index cards, sugar cubes, paper sacks, and popped popcorn. For each pair of kids, provide a sack of popcorn, a sack containing ten sugar cubes, and twelve index cards. Be sure to have extra popcorn to munch on later!

THE FUN

Invite kids to form pairs. Hand each pair a sack of sugar cubes, a sack of popcorn, and twelve index cards. Say: **You and your friend have a special challenge. You're going to build two towers: one using popcorn and index cards, and the other using sugar cubes and index cards. You must use six index cards for each tower. Ready? Build those towers!**

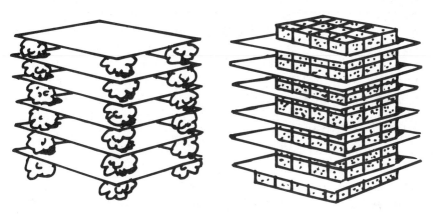

THE FELLOWSHIP

Allow time for partners to build both towers. Then ask:
- **Which towers were easier to build? Why?**
- **Which towers will stand stronger and sturdier? Why?**
- **How does solid support keep buildings from crumbling down?**
- **How can supporting a friend keep your friendship from falling apart?**

Say: **You know, building a sturdy tower is a lot like building a strong, sturdy friendship. The support we give friends when times are tough helps keep our friendships strong. The Bible has a lot to say about supporting our friends.** Read aloud Luke 10:25-37. Then ask:
- **In what ways did the Samaritan support the hurt man?**
- **Do you think the Samaritan and the hurt man became good friends? Explain.**
- **Because of the way he was treated by the Samaritan, do you think the hurt man understood friendship better? What do you think he learned?**
- **In what ways can you support your friends?**

Say: **Supporting friends makes for strong foundations in our friendships. Without supporting our friends, our friendships may tumble.** Have kids blow on their popcorn towers to tumble them. **But when we support our friends with kindness, understanding, and faith, we know our friendships will stand strong!** Have kids gently blow on their sugar cube towers—they should remain standing.

Eggbert

Friendly Focus: Real friends care about you all the time.

Scripture: Proverbs 17:17

Overview: In this fun outdoor game, kids will laugh and learn about caring.

Preparation: You'll need a Bible, several soft towels, and two raw eggs for each student. Before class, use a marker to draw a happy face on each egg. Make sure to tell kids to wear old clothing or paint shirts. This game is best suited for a sunny day outdoors.

THE FUN

Have kids form pairs, and hand each pair a raw egg. Instruct kids to line up facing their partners for an old-fashioned egg toss. Be sure kids are standing about two feet apart.

Say: **This game is all about caring for your egg, whom we'll affectionately call Eggbert. When I say "toss," carefully toss Eggbert to your partner. Then each of you take one small step backward. Each time I say "toss," toss Eggbert to your partner and take a small step backward. We'll see how far you can carefully toss and catch Eggbert.**

Continue until only one or two eggs remain unbroken. Then hand one of those pairs of kids each a soft towel. Have them repeat the game using the towels to carefully catch Eggbert. Encourage the rest of the kids to join in calling "toss." If there's time, allow each pair of kids to try the egg toss using the soft towels.

THE FELLOWSHIP

Following the egg toss, ask:

• **How did treating Eggbert with care help keep him from breaking?**

• **How did the soft towels help even more?**

● What would have happened if you hadn't been careful with Eggbert?

● In what way was this game like treating your friends with loving care?

Say: **Did you know that real friends should care for you all the time? That means that even when things are really rough, good friends won't leave. They'll stick with you and care for you through all the hard times. The Bible has wise words about caring for friends.** Ask a volunteer to read aloud Proverbs 17:17. Then ask:

● Why does a good friend care for you all the time and not just when it's handy?

● In what ways can you "hang in there" and care for your friends?

Say: **It's not good to show you care just sometimes—good friends care for each other all the time! Now show your partners you care by giving them a high five for the great jobs they did in caring for Eggbert!**

Forgive Me?

Friendly Focus: Real friends love you even when you disappoint them.

Scripture: Luke 22:54-62; John 21:15-17

Overview: Kids will make delicious treats and discover that love is the sweetest friend-maker of all.

Preparation: You'll need Bibles, crackers, plastic knives, paper towels, and an assortment of toppers such as raisins, peanuts, olives, apple slices, cheese spread, peanut butter, and jelly.

THE FUN

Set out crackers, plastic knives, paper towels, and the selection of toppers. Have kids form pairs. Then say: **Today we're going to make special treats for our friends. I'll give each of you a cracker, and you can decorate it with any of the goodies on the table. Then you'll have a chance to present your treat to your friend.**

Hand each student a cracker on a paper towel. Allow time for kids to make their special treats. Then have kids set the treats on the paper towels in front of them.

Say: **Give the treat you made to your partner, but don't gobble it up yet.** Pause for kids to switch treats. Then ask:

● **Was your treat what you expected? Explain.**

● **How could you have prepared a treat that would be exactly what your partner wanted?**

● **In what ways is forgiving your partner for not making exactly the right treat the same as loving a friend who disappoints you?**

● **How does love strengthen a friendship?**

Say: **Just as we may not have pleased our partners with our cracker treats, sometimes we all do things that hurt or disappoint our friends. Often we're not even aware of what we've said or done. It's important for friends to be honest and to be loving. Let's read about a time Jesus still loved a friend even after that friend disappointed him.** Read aloud Luke 22:54-62 and John 21:15-17. Then ask:

● **Why did Jesus forgive Peter?**

● **How did Peter feel when Jesus forgave him?**

● **In what ways can you show more love to your friends?**

Say: **We've learned that strong friendships are built on love. Now let's make a second treat. Ask your partner what kind of cracker he or she would like, then make the cracker and present it to your friend.**

Not Again!

Friendly Focus: Real friends forgive each other.

Scripture: Matthew 18:21-22

Overview: In this cooperative, interactive game, kids will learn that the same friend can make a mistake more than once, but that real friends forgive each other.

Preparation: You'll need a Bible, rulers, wooden blocks or boxes that are wider than the width of the ruler, masking tape, a watch or timer, paper, and a pencil.

THE FUN

Make a fifteen- to twenty-inch masking tape line across the floor in the center of the room. Form two groups. Have each group stand single file at opposite ends of the line. The lines should be facing each other.

Choose one line to begin, and give the first person in that line the ruler and block. That person is the Runner. The last person in the opposite line is the Scorekeeper. Give the Scorekeeper the paper and pencil.

Demonstrate how to hold the ruler straight in front of you with the block balanced on the end of the ruler. Explain that the Runner must quickly walk along the line, staying on the line at all times, while balancing the block on the end of the ruler.

When the Runner reaches the first person in the other line, he or she hands the block and ruler to that person, then goes back to the end of his or her original line to help cheer on the next Runner. The Scorekeeper records every "mistake" made—every time a Runner from either line drops the block or steps off the line.

The object of the game is to have everyone in both lines have a turn as the Runner within seven minutes.

Start the timer, and begin the game. Continue the game until everyone has a turn as a Runner. After the game, have the Scorekeeper add the mistakes from each group. The number of mistakes will determine the "score." The game is "won" if the players have all had a turn being the Runner within the seven-minute time limit and the score adds up to fourteen or another multiple of seven (twenty-one, twenty-eight, thirty-five, and so on). If you have a smaller group, set the time limit for less than seven minutes; for a larger group, increase the number. Just make sure the scores add up to a multiple of the number you chose as the time limit.

Tell kids that they may hoot, holler, and clap if they win; or moan, groan, and pretend to cry if they lose. Have the Scorekeeper announce the results, and enjoy the moment by leading kids in the appropriate response.

THE FELLOWSHIP

Gather kids into a circle. Ask:

- **What was it like to be the Runner?**
- **How did it feel having all of your mistakes recorded?**
- **What were you thinking when you saw the Runners making the same mistakes over and over?**

Say: **Jesus gives us some guidelines for what to do when our friends make mistakes over and over.** Read aloud Matthew 18:21-22. Then say: **Think of how many mistakes we all made in our game today. If we think of our total score as times to forgive, we didn't come anywhere near the seventy-seven times Jesus talks about. For most of us, forgiving a friend even one time may seem hard!**

But remember, real friends forgive each other—not just once, but again and again. Close your time together with a prayer thanking God for his forgiveness and asking him to help you follow his example.

Circle Up, Circle Open

Friendly Focus: Real friends don't shut each other out.

Scripture: Acts 9:26-31

Overview: By trying to keep a friendship circle intact, kids will learn that circles of friendship can offer support or exclude friends who need support.

Preparation: You'll need Bibles.

THE FUN

Have kids hold hands and form a large circle. If you have more than ten students, form two circles. Select one person to remain outside the circle.

Say: **We'll call the person outside the circle Saul. Saul will walk around the outside of the circle and suddenly try to break through the hands of two of the kids forming the circle.** Caution kids not to hold hands too tightly and not to break through too forcefully.

Explain that if the breakthrough is successful, Saul will change places with one of the kids who allowed the breakthrough.

If the breakthrough isn't successful, Saul will run around the circle while everyone counts loudly to ten. At ten, Saul will stop and tap the nearest person, who will then join Saul outside the circle. That person will be called Barnabas.

Saul and Barnabas will link arms and begin the game again. If they're successful in breaking through the circle, Saul will again change places with one of the kids, and a new Saul will join Barnabas outside the circle.

If the breakthrough isn't successful, Saul and Barnabas will run around the circle to the count of ten. When they stop at ten, they tap the nearest person in the circle, and the three start the circle walk again. The group outside the circle can get as large as necessary to break through the circle. Continue the game until everyone has had a chance to be either Saul or Barnabas.

THE FUN

Have kids form pairs or trios, and give each group an inflated balloon and a blindfold. Say: **With your partner, decide who will be blindfolded first.** Help kids with the blindfolds, if necessary. **Now, face your partner and place the balloon between your bellies. You'll have to lean together to hold it in place. When I say "go," you and your partner will have one minute to collect a treat from each bag.** Point out the bags in each corner. **If you drop your balloon, stop, pick it up, and put it back between your bellies before you continue. The "sighted" partners will have to give good instructions to the blindfolded partners. Ready? Go!**

After a minute, call time, have partners switch roles, and play again. Then collect the blindfolds, and have kids hold their candies.

THE FELLOWSHIP

Ask:

- **When you were blindfolded, what helped you get the treats?**

- **When you weren't blindfolded, what helped you get the treats?**

- **In both situations, how did you show that you trusted your partner?**

Say: **Whether or not you could see during this game, you had to trust that your partner would work with you. Let's check out a Bible story about some friends who trusted God.** Have a volunteer read aloud Daniel 3:16-28. Ask:

- **How did Shadrach, Meshach, and Abednego show they trusted God?**

- **When are times you trust God?**

● How can you be a "Shadrach, Meshach, or Abednego" to your friends?

Say: **When real friends trust God, the rewards are sweet! Let's eat our sweet treats now. As you eat each treat, tell your partner one way you can show your friends that you trust God.**

Banded Together

Friendly Focus: Real friends help you obey God.

Scripture: John 15:12-17

Overview: In this activity, kids will work together to get a job done and realize the importance of helping each other follow the rules.

Preparation: You'll need Bibles and one rubber band for each person. You'll also need to provide some simple supplies that kids will use to perform the tasks listed below. Just before class, set out the supplies.

THE FUN

ave kids form groups of no more than four, and have each group form a circle. Give each person a rubber band, and show kids how to slip the rubber bands over their right wrists. Say: **Now slip your left hand through your neighbor's rubber band, so your group members are all banded together at their wrists.**

When each group is "joined together," say: **Now I'll give your group a job to do. You'll have to keep your wrists joined together while you complete your task. This isn't a race, but you must completely finish your job. When your group finishes the task, sit down but keep your wrists banded together. Ready?**

Give each group one of the following simple tasks:
● Dust the tables and bookcases.
● Sweep the floor.
● Give another group a big hug.
● Give each group member a high five.
● Get drinks of water for each member of another group.
● Make a birthday card for someone in another group.

THE FELLOWSHIP

hen each group is sitting, ask:
● Was your task easy or hard to accomplish? Explain.
● What might have happened if one person in your

group had refused to do the task?

Say: **In this game, your group members either pulled against you or worked to help you.** Ask:

● **In real life, how do friends sometimes try to pull us the wrong way?**

Say: **Jesus gave a special command to us. Let's read John 15:12-17 to find out what that was.** Distribute Bibles, and have group members work together to look up the passage and read it aloud. Ask:

● **What was Jesus' command?**

● **What is one thing that a real friend would do to help you follow Jesus' command?**

Say: **Some friends might try to pull us away from God, but real friends help us obey God. When we work together to love each other, it's easier to follow Jesus' commands. In your group, pray and ask God to show you how to help your friends obey God.**

Building Buddies

Friendly Focus: Real friends work together to solve problems.

Scripture: Esther 4:1-17

Overview: In this activity, partners will work together to build graham cracker houses and learn the importance of cooperation.

Preparation: You'll need a Bible, paper plates, graham crackers, marshmallow creme, paper bowls, and plastic knives. You'll also need toppings such as M&M's, cereal, or peanuts.

THE FUN

Have kids form pairs, and give each pair a paper plate, three graham crackers, a cup of marshmallow creme, a bowl of toppings, and a plastic knife. Say: **Put your right hand behind your back. Now, you and your partner will have five minutes to build a graham cracker house. Each person can only use one hand. Ready? Go!**

After five minutes, call time and have kids show off their grand creations. Set the graham cracker houses aside, and have kids form a circle.

THE FELLOWSHIP

Ask:
- What problems did you face when you tried to build your houses?
- How did you solve your problems?
- What did you learn about your partner in this activity?

Say: This activity reminds me of two people in the Bible who had to work together, Esther and Mordecai. Queen Esther was a Jew; however the king didn't know it. One of the king's highest officials, named Haman, didn't like the Jews. He came up with a plan to kill every Jewish person in the whole kingdom! When Esther's cousin Mordecai learned about Haman's wicked plot, he knew he had to act quickly to save his people! Let's read Esther 4:1-17 to find out how Esther and Mordecai worked together to solve their problem. Have a volunteer read aloud Esther 4:1-17. Ask:
- How did Esther and Mordecai work together?
- How is that like the way you and your partner worked together?
- What happens when we work together to solve problems?

Say: Just as you needed your partners to build the houses, Mordecai needed Esther to help carry out his plan. They had to work together to solve a big problem. When real friends work together to solve problems, they come up with tasty solutions! Let's enjoy our graham cracker houses to remind us how great it is to work together.

Broken Bubbles

Friendly Focus: Real friends keep their promises.

Scripture: 1 Samuel 20:42; 2 Samuel 9:1-7

Overview: Kids will participate in a bubble relay and learn the importance of keeping promises.

Preparation: You'll need a Bible, a bottle of bubble solution, and a bubble wand.

THE FUN

Have kids form two groups, and have them line up at opposite sides of the room, facing each other. (If you have more than ten kids, form four groups.) Give the first person in Group One a container of bubble solution and a bubble wand.

Say: (Name of person) **will blow a bubble. Then** (he or she) **will blow the bubble across the room to the first person in Group Two's line, give that person the bubble solution, then stay on Group Two's side.**

The person from Group Two will blow the same bubble back to the next person in Group One. Continue until everyone has blown the bubble and traded sides. If the bubble pops, simply blow a new one and keep going. Ready? Go!

Play until everyone has had a turn to blow a bubble across the room. Then collect the bubble solution and wand.

THE FELLOWSHIP

Gather kids in a circle and ask:
- **What did you notice about the bubbles?**
- **What helped you move the bubbles successfully?**
- **In what ways do these bubbles remind you of promises?**

Say: **It was hard to control the breakable bubbles, and it can be hard to follow through when we make promises. But God wants us to be faithful friends who keep our promises. Let's learn about a promise that David made to his best friend, Jonathan.**

Read aloud 1 Samuel 20:42 and 2 Samuel 9:1-7. Then ask:
- **How did David keep his promise?**
- **Do you think it might have been hard to keep that promise? Explain.**
- **Why did David keep his promise to Jonathan?**

Say: **It can be hard to keep some promises. Sometimes, it seems like it would be easier to just let the promise break, kind of like our bubbles. But real friends keep their promises. Let's blow some more bubbles, then pray and ask God to help us keep our promises.**

Let kids blow a few more bubbles. Then lead the class in a prayer asking for God's help in keeping promises.

Scripture Index